D1562354

QUEER
NEW YORK CITY

2002-2003

PUBLISHER
Jeff Brauer

EDITOR IN CHIEF
Martin Joseph Quinn

DESIGN
Paul Choi

ART
Nelson Quizhpi

PROJECTS DIRECTOR
Pas Niratbhand

STAFF WRITERS
Martin Joseph Quinn, Michael Angelo,
Trevor Soponis

ON YOUR OWN PUBLICATIONS, LLC
Corporate Address:
Brooklyn Navy Yard
Building 120, Suite 207
Brooklyn, NY 11205

Tel: 718.875.9455
Fax: 561.673.2436
Email: oyobooks@yahoo.com

CONTENTS

How to Use This Book

GETTING SPECIFIC

Many places in NYC advertise themselves as one thing when they actually offer so much more. Listed alongside each entry are icons that represent what you can expect at each venue.

DIVE

QUEER NYC RECOMMENDS

PICK-UP JOINT

FOOD

MEN

DRAG

WOMEN

UPSCALE

"A hustle here and a hustle there, New York City is the place where they said, 'Hey babe, take a walk on the wild side.'"

–Lou Reed
Walk on the Wild Side

Introduction

▼

Welcome, queer boys and girls! The purpose of this book is to make you feel at home in our thriving metropolis, whether you are here for a few days on a business trip or have lived here all your life. Our intrepid writers and researchers have visited each site personally, and have covered all five boroughs with insight and experience in order to direct you to the pockets of the city that cater to your interests.

Lesbian and gay bars are great places to chat with old friends or meet new ones. New York is also host to the best dance clubs in the nation, and our dance clubs section will help you decide where to get your groove on. If a beautiful voice and melody excite you, the cabarets and piano bars in the city are top notch, attracting Broadway-level talent. If you're looking to scratch an itch, we've listed the spots to frolic with the hot and horny. For guys and gals looking to meet people with similar interests and learn a thing or two, the community resources section will guide you in the right direction. Whatever your inclination, we've provided the information. Dive in!

Top Queer NYC Lists

TOP GAY BARS
Barracuda
The Cock
Music Box
Chi Chiz
Hannah's Love Lounge

TOP SEX
Ann St. Entertainment Center
West Side Club
82nd Street Club
Unicorn All-Male Cinema

TOP LESBIAN BARS
Ginger's Bar
Rubyfruit Bar & Grill
Henrietta Hudson

TOP COMMUNITY SERVICES
Gay and Lesbian Community
Services Center
Bluestockings Women's Bookstore
Oscar Wilde Bookshop

TOP DANCE CLUBS
Flamingo
Spa
Roxy
Speeed
Heaven

TOP LODGING
Inn on 23rd St.
333 West 88th Associates
Chelsea Pines Inn

TOP CABARETS & PIANO BARS
Danny's Grand Sea Palace
Rose's Turn
Lips
Duplex

Bars

▼

How many times have you heard someone say, "You'll never meet the love of your life in a bar?" They are wrong — people do meet lovers, as well as friends and one-night-stands in bars, especially the lesbian and gay ones. New York has a bar for all tastes. Whether it's bumping against bears at the Dugout, falling in with the in-crowd at Barracuda, checking out baskets at the Cock, making friends at Friend's Tavern, or getting crazy at Crazy Nanny's, you will find your home away from home.

A few simple guidelines: 1. Be nice to the bartenders and bouncers. 2. Be nice to everybody. Keep an open mind. 3. Experiment. If you're a visitor staying in the Midtown area, get yourself on our efficient subway system and check out the Upper East Side. If you've been going to the same East Village bar down the block for five years, it wouldn't kill you to buy someone a drink at one of the many festive Brooklyn watering holes. 4. Have fun. If you're in a bad mood, fake it. 5. Don't be a stranger.

The Abbey

536 Driggs Avenue, Williamsburg, Brooklyn .
Everyday 4pm-4am, 718.599.4400

Williamsburg is even hipper than you thought. Stand on the corner near the Bedford Ave. subway stop and be trampled by hoards of English majors heading out for a couple of beers. An avenue away from this subway stop, The Abbey bustles with cute, young energy seven days a week. It has a bit more of an edge than the other Williamsburg watering holes due to a healthy percentage of queers.

The place definitely has a college feel to it. A London Calling poster hangs by the pool table, near gaggles of animated youngsters sitting in booths. The TV often plays old movies, and one could become mesmerized while in a drunken stupor. The music coming from the jukebox is never boring. Beck, Red House Painters, Rufus, Roots and Muddy Waters share airtime here. If you're out with a straight friend and you're both looking for love in all the wrong places, The Abbey could be the perfect compromise between homo and hetero. As the night marches on, eyes start wandering and strangers start talking to each other. Like most Brooklyn bars, the crowd is laid back, the mix of people is somewhat unpredictable, and anything goes.

The bartenders are always accommodating and knowledgeable. Half the customers drink $3 Lagers anyway, so they have it easy. Everybody is pretty great here, making the Abbey worth a trip on the L.
Your Words: "Bobby, Peter and I have scored here many

times." "It reminds me of when I got drunk every day for a month my last week of college." "When I get bored of my CD collection, I come here for the jukebox."

BARS

Albatross

36-19 24th Avenue @ 37th Street, Astoria, Queens
Everyday 6pm-3am, 718.274.9164

During the past year, there's been a rumor going around that Astoria, Queens is New York's "New Bohemia" neighborhood, following in the footsteps of the Lower East Side, Williamsburg, and pretty much every neighborhood outside of Staten Island. Well, Astoria is not the "New Bohemia." It's the same old boring community we know and love — cheap clothes, great diners, a place to raise a kid. So stop raising our rent!

Smack in the middle of our wonderful community is Albatross, a sleepy dive bar near the BQE. It's pretty much the opposite of bohemian, thank God. Action here revolves around the pool table from open until close. Things can get very intense. A picture of Joan Crawford surrounded by Christmas lights hangs next to a New York Liberty poster on the back wall. Wonder if Joan would appreciate that? Below Joan is an old couch and even older lamp. It looks like some gay kid's basement hideaway. Older gay men and younger lesbians hang out here, along with various billiard aficionados. Jocelyn, the beautiful and vivacious bartender, tells stories of gangs of straight Brazilian girls chasing the 8 ball and getting really competitive. Anything goes here in Astoria.

> "Precious people always tell me, that's a step, a step too far."
>
> **BOY GEORGE**

Mostly everybody knows everybody else here. If a customer went behind the bar and poured her own drink, don't be surprised. It's a good place for a neighbor to have a drink and throw some darts instead of schlepping into Manhattan or waiting on line at nearby Krash.

Your Words: "I don't have to wait in a long line to play pool." "I've drowned my sorrows here and felt better afterwards." "My friend and I can walk a few blocks, sit on the couch in the back, and catch up."

Atlantis 2010

76-19 Roosevelt Avenue, Jackson Heights, Queens
W-Su 10pm-4am, 718.457.3939

Atlantis 2010 is a spacious, fun spot in the heart of Jackson Heights. There's a huge island bar in the middle, and lots of large tables spread across the hardwood floor. Mirrors along the wall make it look even bigger. Statues of naked men around the perimeter of the space and pillars from the bar to the ceiling create a nifty Roman feel. While the other bars in the area are usually cramped, Atlantis has room to move.

The music from the DJ station pumps hard and clear from a quality sound system, but unfortunately there's no dance floor, which probably means no cabaret license. Still, people can't help themselves, moving their feet to some good salsa, house and merengue. The crowd is 21-35, mostly Latin, quiet some nights and raging other nights. Half come with friends, half are alone and looking. The staff is friendly and accommodating. Cabaret Fridays feature drag performers, and Sunday is Gong Show Talent Search night, which can get crazy.

Down the street from Friend's Tavern and The Music Box, Atlantis makes for a good stop on a Queens bar-hopping spree. You can hit all three bars in the same night and see a lot of the same people. If you're there late and hungry from too much drinking, stop at one of the street vendors and chow down on some delicious greasiness. Smack in the middle of lively Queens, Atlantis 2010 is an energetic spot for horsing around and getting down.

Your Words: "A night at all three Jackson Heights bars leaves me high and dry." "The Gong Show there is too much."

The Bar

68 2nd Avenue @ 4th Street, Manhattan
Everyday 4pm to 4am

The Bar is a good all-purpose joint. The atmosphere is low-key, and makes for a good place to drown sorrows, hang out with a friend, or chat with a stranger.

It's rarely packed, but there's usually a decent crowd of neighborhood regulars, NYUers, hardcore pool players and the occasional out-of-town boy on the make. During the past year, visitors include a Montana truckstop owner, a few wealthy-yet-troubled ex's, and bartenders from nearby watering holes. Straight tourists often wander in, and sometimes they stay. The not-too-comfortable benches around the perimeter of the pool table serve as a good perch for people-watching.

The bartenders are among the friendliest in New York. They smile when they serve, and chat with you when you're bored. Once, while killing time near Christmas, the bartender waxed prophetic with the local crowd about Cher, good looking men and life in general — these are people who've been through life once already.

The walls are covered with caricatures of Moby, Bjork and David Bowie, a South Park poster, and Ken Burns' Jazz series prints. The jukebox, like all East Village jukeboxes, is diverse, although "Sexbomb" by Tom Jones and Madonna always seem to be playing.

The Bar is a prime place to have a drink after work, or to down a few drinks before dancing. Proximity to the adjacent Boiler Room and down-the-street Fat Cock 29 is convenient if you're in the mood for hopping around. Whether alone or accompanied, The Bar is a great place to feel comfortable in your own skin.

Your Words: "A good place to pick up down-to-earth guys." "The best dive bar in the East Village."

Bar 4

444 7th Avenue @ 15th Street, Park Slope, Brooklyn
Everyday 4pm-4am, 718.832.9800

One cool aspect of Bar 4 is they actually have a drink menu. It makes it easy for an indecisive, adventurous person to try something new. Lots of people opt for the martinis, including chocolate, lemon drop or sour apple. How about a lambic cocktail? The bloody marys are awesome. The bar has a café feel to it, so coffee and espresso is served also.

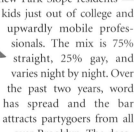

The crowd at Bar 4 is a good reflection of new Park Slope residents — kids just out of college and upwardly mobile professionals. The mix is 75% straight, 25% gay, and varies night by night. Over the past two years, word has spread and the bar attracts partygoers from all over Brooklyn. The decoration is simple and swank. Lots of pillows rest on benches, every table is candlelit, and red velvety curtains blow from the wind. Happy Hour is a short 6 to 7:30 (what if I get off work at

5?). Local DJs set up right inside the front window and spin lounge, house, world beat, and whatever from Wednesday to Saturday. It's nothing revolutionary or unique, but Bar 4 is a cool place for after-dinner drinks on the Slope.

Your Words: "Go to Prospect Park, lay out in the sun, throw a frisbee around, and then come here for a martini." "Finally there's a place on 7th Ave. where a young, cute lesbian like me can hang out."

Bar d'O

29 Bedford Street @ Downing Street, Manhattan
M-F 7pm-2am, Sa-Su 7pm-4am, 212.627.1580

Five years ago, trying to find a straight man in a gay bar would have been as fruitful a venture as trying to find meaning in a Stallone movie. But times, they are a'changin'. Along with our new politically correct, it's-okay-to-be-gay mentality, a new batch of mixed bars are making their way into the large metropolises across the land. Bar d'O is one of these brotherly establishments. Although considered to be mainly a cruisy gay bar, at any time a large portion of breeders can be found scattered amidst the more exclusive homos of the West Village.

The cabaret show on Tuesdays, Saturdays and Sundays, which features some of NYC's most talented and tantalizing drag queens, attracts a larger straight clientele every week. The only real exception to this cultural phenomenon is Monday night's lesbian night. The crowd on these nights is usually limited to women, with a smattering of gay men here and there. Mirrors align every wall in the joint, and the small room lined with cushy black leather couches and ottomans is as void of light as the second circle of hell.

Bar d'O is all about successful, eclectic and beautiful people. A night in this place will please the eyes and ears, but could cause a major depletion in one's finances. Beers are five dollars, while drinks range from $6-$12. Expensive single malts like Macellan are featured nightly. Even the deejay spinning New World music gives off a very cultured vibe. Forget Britney — think sitars and mandolins.

While the primping and pretensions of the upper class are always apparent, tolerance and diversity are the most prevalent flavors in Bar d'O, an attractive quality in a world still fraught with bigotry. Some say that curiosity killed the cat. So, why don't you come here to see just how curious are the Dockers-clad boys lounging throughout the room.

Your Words: "A chic and modern mix of the best that the West Village has to offer." "So many young straight boys...makes me feel like a horny teenager all over again."

Barracuda

275 W 22nd Street @ 8th Avenue, Manhattan
Everyday 4pm-4am, 212.645.8613

Barracuda delivers a touch of retro-bohemia in Chelsea. It looks like the set of an Esquivel music video, if there were such a thing. The space is divided into two parts. The front bar is where guys on the prowl hang out, sitting on bleachers or milling around the three tables. The back opens up to an inviting room with couches, and a red velvet pool table matching the red chairs around the room. Red and yellow illuminated spheres hang from the ceiling, and the bar is backed by a trippy mosaic of colored panels. It's kitschy, colorful and cute, and one could be happy sipping and chatting for hours. Arms are lazily draped over armrests, and gay boys in their twenties slouch in their seats and gossip. Everybody comes here sooner or later for good reason. It's a good place to meet people. The relaxed, cheery vibe puts people in a good mood.

The best drag queens NYC has to offer appear here — Girlina, Flotilla Debarge, and Candis Cayne will have you rolling in the aisles. There's never a cover, although they could probably get away with one. The DJs serve up eclectic fare every night, and occasional musical performances entertain the masses. Alternative rock hero Bob Mould sang here a couple of years ago. Barracuda can be an unpredictable experience in a predictable neighborhood. A typical scene at Barracuda: Ben Hur on the television, Nathan Lane sitting at the bar, a female DJ playing a trip-hop set, and a handful of semi-drunks chatting away loudly. You'll return two nights in a row, since you'll have such a good time. Barracuda manages to be fabulous without being snooty, not an easy accomplishment.

Your Words: "Barracuda is timeless. You feel like you're partying in a different decade every time you go." "If you're too lazy to go to a club, but too restless to stay home, go to Barracuda and chill."

Barrage

401 W 47th Street @ 9th Avenue, Manhattan
Everyday 4pm-4am, 212.586.9390

The walls of Barrage are covered with magazine ads — Guess, Abercrombie, Versace. Most of the ads feature a scantily clad male model. From practically open to close, Barrage is packed with men who attain to this archetype. Some of them succeed quite well. If muscle boys and cute prepsters turn you on, you could have fun just squeezing between them on your way to the bathroom at this tiny, very popular midtown watering hole.

People are always talking up a storm here. A hundred people sound like a thousand in the small space. It's not difficult to join in the conversation. Half the bar is covered with benches and stools, and everybody slouches and chats with the ease of old pals. Friends come together, but many boys come alone and don't want to be. Working boys fill the place up during happy hour, often with a loosened tie or knapsack. A Chelsea-ish crowd descends upon Barrage at night. At all times, it can

> "If they think I'm straight or gay, it's great — at least they think I'm going to bed with somebody."
>
> **BRUCE WEBER**

be a fight to get to the bar for a drink. If you're one to worry that you're destination won't be swarmed by cuties, Barrage is a best bet for constant crowds.

Most everybody has a cigarette in their hands, and you wonder whether the goldfish in the fishbowls at the bar are suffering from the second hand smoke. There's no jukebox, but the music is pretty eclectic, ranging from pop to swing to techno.

The atmosphere is generally social and cheery. Adjacent to the Calvary Christian Church, Barrage has attracted a religious following of its own.

Your Words: "My gay and straight coworkers love Happy Hour." "I come here after rehearsal."

The Boiler Room

86 E 4th Street @ 2nd Avenue, Manhattan
Everyday 4pm-4am, 212.254.7536

Once the hub of the East Village bar scene, The Boiler Room has more competition these days but still packs a cool crowd. It shares the same clientele as its neighbor The Bar, but is more spacious and a bit livelier.

The décor of The Boiler Room has gotten snazzier over the years. Near the windows, there are sofas where hard benches used to be. On the opposite side of the bar, there's a semi-private nook with lamps and velvet curtains, a good place for a private conversation away from the milieu. Lighting is dim but not dark. The atmosphere has become more lounge, less edge. Prices are slightly higher than in the past, but still average for the surrounding area.

On weekends, The Boiler Room is standing room only. Sometimes it takes a while to order a drink. Smack in the middle of the space is a pool table, and boys form a perimeter around the action, cruising each other while pretending to watch the 8-ball. In a partly-concealed corner near the door, there are leather couches and a large bench. If you're looking to meet someone, sit on one of the couches and wait. Within 15 minutes you'll have company.

The jukebox selection isn't rotated very often, but it's always filled with happy pop music to keep the crowd going. A few times a bartender has switched off the jukebox to play a CD behind the bar, which annoys some customer who spent his hard-earned dollar to listen to Bjork. The television silently sits above the bar, usually turned to regular prime-time fare.

The Boiler Room is a failsafe choice for fun any night of the week. It's a good place to end up with a date after pigging out at one of the many surrounding cheap eateries, or if you're alone, relaxed and on the prowl.

Your Words: "It's a low key watering hole, good for shooting the breeze with a cute stranger." "Definitely don't have to dress up for the Boiler Room. I go there after work with pals sometimes."

Boots & Saddle

76 Christopher Street @ 7th Avenue, Manhattan
Everyday 8am-4am, 212.929.9684

Boots & Saddle has an intimidating exterior. It looks like a place where rough, leathery men spit on the floor and ostracize newcomers.

The bar retains some of the masculinity from days of yore. A large hitching post stands in the middle of the small bar, and the walls are covered with imitation Tom of Finland drawings. The bathroom is cramped, with rubber adorning the walls, a trough barely long enough for two, and a blackboard with no chalk hanging over the trough. Other aspects of the bar are tame. The jukebox houses a who's who of stereotypical gay icons, from Patti to Barbara to Madonna remixes. There's even a little stuffed Pikachu sitting over the bar.

The crowd is old-school homo, with the majority of men donning jeans and a beard. During the week, Boots is scattered with hard-drinking locals and groups of friends meeting after work. On the weekend, the small space becomes crowded and less cruisy than one would think. But if you like your men a little older, handsome, and a bit gruff, this could be home away from home. There's a historical vibe here also, attracting more than the occasional tourist.

Boots and Saddle has been around for 26 years and shows no signs of slowing down. Within five blocks of Stonewall, Ty's, and Hangar Bar and across the way from the lively Duplex, Boots is a good stop on a West Village pub crawl. Or plant your ass on the hitching post and enjoy the scenery.

Your Words: "Bump bellies with the best of them." "A good representation of the old style West Village."

Bridge Bar

309 E 60th Street @ 2nd Avenue, Manhattan
Everyday 4pm-4am, 212.223.9104

If you can brave the fumes and congestion emanating from the Queensboro Bridge, and then actually find the hole-in-the-wall Bridge Bar, congratulate yourself because you're in for a treat. It's a neighborhood bar in the best sense of the word, where the old-timers saddle up to the bar next to the occasional tight-shirted youngster.

> "I don't mind straight people, as long as they act gay in public."
>
> **DENNIS RODMAN**

Near the entrance, there are hanging paper streamers, Herb Ritts posters and some well placed mirrors to distract you from noticing the snug surroundings. Once you head toward the back of the bar, the space opens up enough for a pool table and a lounge area with a few couches. Adorable Michael is quick to fill up your drink or introduce you to the guy sitting next to you. Happy hour runs from 4pm to 9pm and nothing's too expensive. The music comes from either the oldies-filled jukebox or random CDs from the bar, anything from Madonna to Basement Jaxx to Aretha.

A crowd of regulars shuffles out around 9pm weeknights and it's hit-or-miss whether it fills up again toward the wee hours. Weekends bring a full house, and Sundays it's Arabian Night, complete with belly dancers. One of the few bars over on the quiet East Side, the Bridge Bar is a prime place for a good laugh and an honest drink.

Your Words: "They make a nice Manhattan." "...removed from the cattiness of other neighborhoods."

BS East

113-24 Queens Blvd., near 76th Avenue, Forest Hills, Queens Everyday 4pm-4am, 718.263.0300

So you're visiting your grandparents in Queens. You love them, but they're driving you crazy. You're starting to feel claustrophobic in the cramped, cluttered apartment. Where do you go to escape? There aren't many gay bars out here around Forest Hills, so BS East draws all types and ages from the surrounding community. If you're sick of competing with the pretty boys in that other borough, knock a few back here with some regular dudes.

Similar to its sister bar on Third Ave. in Manhattan, BS shows the latest videos on over 20 monitors around the bar. The two-for-one happy hour draws a decent crowd most evenings, and classic rock night on Friday has queer boys digging up their Zeppelin T-shirts. There's also a pool tournament on Mondays, and DJ Ricky playing those videos while men wet their moustaches with 2-for-1 drinks. Hunky go-go boys on Saturday will have you spinning. Like most outer borough bars, there's no hard-core cruise scene going on here, but strangers leave with strangers all the time. If you're in the mood for martinis and sparkling banter, head elsewhere. If you wanna hang with some good guys and pound back some brewskies, sneak out while your grandma's watching Regis and come down to BS East.

Your Words: "A place to meet new people and be yourself. What else do you need from a bar?" "I come out here from Long Island all the time. I love it."

BS New York

405 3rd Avenue @ 29th Street, Manhattan
Everyday noon-4am, 212.684.8376

Seemingly miles from any other gay bar, BS New York is the only true music video bar in NYC. Yes, going out of your house to watch music videos is kind of hokey, but the DJ at BS East also works for Rock America and has access to the latest and greatest clips. For some reason, it seems natural to drink a screwdriver and watch consecutive N'Sync, old Erasure and St. Etienne videos. And if you're alone, you don't have to stare out into space waiting for someone to talk to you. You're watching a George Michael video!

Bars where the owner is present and involved are usually the most friendly, and BS is no exception. Marco and the bartenders know all the regulars and treat them well. Since there isn't another queer bar for 20 blocks, the loyal regulars are plentiful. Fridays and Sundays are the busiest nights, but there's always a decent crowd here, made up of 20-40 year old blue and white collar guys, some East Villagers and music video fans. It's a great place to shoot some pool or lose yourself in video games.

Lots of NY bars claim to be "The Gay Cheers," but BS might come the closest (although it's difficult to imagine Diane Chambers watching ATeens videos). Like the Hangar in the West Village and Phoenix in the East, BS is a comfortable watering hole for the surrounding community.

Your Words: "...nice guys and good conversation." "They don't play videos on MTV anymore, so it's the only place I get to see music videos."

Candle Bar

309 Amsterdam Avenue, Between 74th & 75th Street, Manhattan
Everyday 2pm-4am, 212.874.9155

Amidst the ephemeral and trendy clubs of the booming Upper West Side, Candle Bar has endured the test of time. Like a Dollar Discount Store in the Manhattan Mall, this cheap little neighborhood bar has served the gay community for 30 years. The amenities often associated with gay bars (DJs, dance floors, lounge areas, drag shows) are not available here, but the seediness and friendliness of the place preserves the thriving business of this little hole in the wall.

Stone mosaic candleholders, collages and decoupage paintings line the bar and liquor shelves. Most of the works celebrate iconic male appendages of various shapes and sizes. Hanging in the eaves above the bar and pool table are paper plate snowflakes made by patrons in the winter and then sold in the spring. All proceeds are donated to the Matthew Shepherd fund. Local NYC artist and bartender Arthur Wimberley specializes in garbage, and his candleholders consist of stones and pebbles from Fire Island. The chandeliers were made from discarded plastic water bottles and filled with Christmas tree lights. He finds beauty in the least likely places.

Candle Bar is one of the few bars in New York City that allows its customers to leave with some spare cash left over. Serving the city with its longest happy hour, the bartenders serve $2 domestic beers and bargain mixed drinks from 2pm-9pm daily and from 2pm-midnight on Mondays. Even without the discount, beers and drinks range from only $3 to a mere $4.50. Themed nights also offer customers more drink for their buck. "Rican Night" on Thursdays offers $2.50 Bacardi drinks. Saturday wine nights feature $2 glasses. And, every Sunday, patrons can ease their post-Saturday hangovers with $2.50 Bloody Marys.

There's nothing fancy about Candle Bar, especially in comparison to the sleek, loungy spots opening up around town. However, cheap drinks and cheap men give the clientele plenty of reasons to keep coming back.

Your Words: "Charming. Diverse. Absolutely comfortable." "This place is nothing like what you would expect of an Upper West Side bar. It's a pleasant surprise."

Chase Bar–Hell's Kitchen

359 W 54th Street, Between 8th & 9th Avenues, Manhattan
Everyday 6pm-2am, 212.582.2200

Combine two parts ambiance, two parts class and one part Cher. Mix well and garnish with a few gay boys. What you'll have is a little taste of the Chase Bar in Hell's Kitchen. Although much smaller than the midtown original, Chase is still abundant with the chic and trendy atmosphere and clientele for which its predecessor is known.

Unlike many of the city's gay bars, Chase makes no secret of its gay affiliation. In addition to the rainbow flag waving proudly above the front door, the large, brightly lit front window displays all that Chase has to offer. The elegant and eye-catching turquoise marble bar illuminated by an art deco/crystal chandelier is often surrounded by an eclectic and hip group of men. The after-theater and after-dinner crowd are here in droves, and stargazing is also a possibility. Chase attracts the likes of NYC stars and businessmen with its famous martinis and cosmopolitans, which come in many different flavors and are often featured as nightly specials.

At the bottom of a spiral staircase, Chase's basement offers patrons a cozy little nook to chat, relax and smooch in. This area, however, should not be considered a rich man's backroom. There is nothing shady about the place. The bright blues of the tiled tabletops and stools, the soft, blue satin couches and the bright lighting give the downstairs the feel of a sanctuary. Since the majority of patrons arrive coupled, very little cruising opportunities await you here.

Chase is a great place to wind down an evening. In fact, many of the midtown Chase clientele finish their night off here. If the affordable nightcaps ($5-7) aren't enough to attract you, the tremendously pleasant and welcoming staff and luminescent architecture will make the trip worthwhile.

Your Words: "Ambiance...ambiance...ambiance. Need I say more?" "Refreshing...a grope-free gay bar."

Chase Midtown

255 W 55th Street, Between 7th & 8th Avenues, Manhattan
Nightly until 4am, 212.333.3400

Chase Midtown is one of many swank lounges that have sprung up in New York City in the past 10 years. While most of the lounge set is hereto-dominated, Chase is unabashedly queer. The place has an airy gallery feel, with strategically placed candles, hardwood floors, clean light-colored walls and a DJ spinning ambient techno.

The vibe is usually relaxed, but not entirely free of pretension. The bulk of Chase's clientele is twentysomething and while the occasional dyke might wander in, it's very male. Some of the younger guys tend to line the wall, hoping to be noticed. Most of the guys who hang out here look like the boys in an *Out* fashion spread. No love handles here. The Chase crowd largely fits the image of 21st century queers on television — beautiful young athletic types who made the transition to adulthood with nary a blemish. There's little cross-generational mixing here, and older guys may not feel so comfortable.

The interior of Chase is impeccable. One wall has an ornate tile shelf serving as a drink rest. The barstools have a Swiss aerodynamic look, which reflect the level of care and planning that went into designing the bar. There's also a backroom with darker lighting and couches, good for conversation. Chase also sports a downstairs lounge area open on weekends, and can be rented out for private functions. Drinks are moderately priced.

Talk to any two people about Chase, and you'll get two entirely different stories about the place — Swank lounge-set, or Dionysian dick-palace. There seems to be enough flexibility to accommodate different tastes. Chase is also a young establishment, and could evolve in any number of different directions over time.

Your Words: "It's a good scene, really classy." "It's cruisy, but a good place to meet guys. I'm actually in a serious relationship with someone I met here."

Chi Chiz

135 Christopher Street @ Hudson Street, Manhattan
Everyday 2pm-4am, 212.462.0027

Formerly a Chinese restaurant with the same name, Chi Chiz may be the friendliest bar on Christopher Street. When you walk in, turn around and check out the etching above the window. It's one of the nicest pieces of art in a NYC bar. Look to your left and you may see Mike the owner greeting everyone who walks in the door. Plant yourself on a stool, order a drink, and before long you'll be shooting the breeze with someone. Chi Chiz is truly a community bar where outsiders also feel welcome.

The interior is simple and cozy. Tables sit across from

the bar in front, original artwork covers the walls, and cushioned benches surround the pool table in back. Young men of color make up 95% of the mix, and while the friendly atmosphere attracts many locals, travelers from Philly, D.C. and elsewhere make Chi Chiz their destination. A business crowd filters in during the two-for-one happy hour, and things get tight and cruisy on weekend nights. Boys also come around before and after the drag shows at Two Potato a few doors down. Chi Chiz hosts regular benefits for AIDS-related causes — fashion shows, musical performances, and pool tournaments — and devotes more energy and resources to charity than most bars.

There's an appetizer menu for when you're hungry and too lazy and/or drunk to walk to one of the kajillion eateries in the Village. Mozzarella sticks taste so good after five vodkas on the rocks. Chi Chiz is the kind of place where you'll probably want to stay awhile.

> "He's here, he's queer, I'm buying him a beer."
>
> **ALEXANDER on QUEER AS FOLK**

Your Words: "...laid back and dark boys..."

The Cock

186 Avenue A @ 12th Street, Manhattan
Everyday 4pm-2am, 212.946.1871

Amidst the forced repression and misguided "quality-of-life" laws of the Giuliani administration stands a proud, erect Cock. Occasionally closed by the cops due to raunchy behavior, the Cock fights back every night with insane amateur strip shows, creative DJs and well, good old-fashioned raunchy behavior.

Painted on the huge mirror that dominates the décor is an ejaculating, plump penis, just in case some patrons don't get the idea. Along the right side of the bar, chatty customers spend the night getting to know each other on cushioned benches, graced with the glow of candlelight. On the left, the diligent bartenders are lean, muscular, and usually aren't wearing much of anything. Drinks are expensive but always strong. Behind the bar, a different DJ every night spins everything from 80's R&B to deep house to diva dance beats to glam, and the selection is always eclectic and fun.

The bathrooms are a story unto themselves. There's usually a line for the private bathroom. Couples often venture in for a private moment. The other bathroom consists of a broken down sink when you first walk in, two adjacent urinals in the middle, and a floor-to-ceiling mirror to the right. The gentleman relieving himself on the right can furtively glance in the mirror to view his neighbor's manhood. Childish maybe, but popular. Many interesting conversations, sometimes without words, take place while waiting.

And then there's the backroom. Once the setting for orgiastic frenzy before the mayoral clampdown, the room now resembles a sauna without the steam. Benches align the walls, and men idle, stroke, flirt, glare, but generally don't touch each other. Most of the time.

All elements of the Cock provide the best possible atmosphere for horny freaks. It's become somewhat infamous, and attracts a few tourists, the occasional Chelsea queen, and lots of juicy East Village boys. Put on something comfortable and go crazy.

Your Words: "It's addicting. I end up staying here for hours every time I come." "The best place to come if you want to get laid."

Crazy Nanny's

21 7th Avenue South @ Leroy Street, Manhattan
Everyday 4pm-4am, 212.366.6312

Although Crazy Nanny's is predominantly a lesbians-of-color establishment, as a pale white dyke you will feel more than comfortable here. During the week it's a great place to relax and hang out with locals of all ages, and the younger crowd bumps, grinds and flirts on the weekend. It's mostly cruisy on the weekends, but a cutey might hit on you any time, and you can never tell. In general, there are no wallflowers here.

The jukebox is filled with all the Sade you could ever ask for. DJs spin from Thursday through Saturday, playing an array of hip-hop and dance. Dancing at Crazy Nanny's is unpretentious, no-holds-barred mania, like an out-of-control house party. The dance floor is small and intimate, and there aren't any blinding club lights. Everyone has a smile on her face. Often events like Reggae Dance contest and Butch/Femme Ball will pop up on the weekends, so be prepared to compete.

When you get tired of dancing, head to one of the lounge areas and find someone to snuggle with. Or go to the downstairs bar and play video games, or strike up a game of pool. The bartenders are nice and chatty, not to mention quite cute. Behind the bar a sign reads "Resuscitation Equipment Is Available With the Bartender Behind the Bar," and that will probably put you at ease.

The drinks are normally priced for a West Village bar — try one of the Bartender Signature drinks for a kick. Overall this is a great place to cruise, hang out or just get completely crazy, hence the name.

Your Words: "I can be myself here. Myself being a wild, dancing fool." "I met my girlfriend here over two years ago. We still come all the time."

> "It's not that I don't like penises. It's just that I don't like them on men."
>
> **LEA DELARIA**

Cubbyhole

281 W 12th Street @ W 4th Street, Manhattan
M-F 4pm-4am, Sa-Su 2pm-2am, 212.243.9041

Yay! Cubbyhole makes drinking fun. Maybe the only bar in 12 states where you can sit on cartoon character barstools, Cubbyhole draws an attractive crowd with good music and the friendliest staff you'll ever find.

If your kid were a drinker, you'd take her here. The bright and multicolored flowers painted on the outside windows attract myriad lesbians and straights nightly. Once a children's room, this renovated bar retains the playfulness and kitsch that would inhabit a kid's play space. Seaweed, goldfish, Christmas balls and paper lamps dangle from the ceiling, and stools animated with various Bugs Bunny & Co. characters line the bar. Cubbyhole, through all its quirkiness, has a homey feel of an eccentric grandmother's house decorated with all those gifts that most would pitch, but she adores.

Even when packed to the brim, the bar staff makes Mary Lou Retton seem like she's frowning. It's good to have happy people around when you're drinking. The huge, delicious martinis are one of the many drink specialties featured nightly, and every Saturday evening (from 8:30 to 10pm) for five dollars, any patron can enjoy an all-you-can-drink special. If you're starved, take advantage of the large number of take-out menus and wash down some grub with one of the many beers on tap. If Daffy Duck were real, he'd love this place.

Your Words: "It looks kind of wacky, but Cubbyhole is simply a good quality neighborhood bar." "It's a refreshing change from dark bars that smell like your basement."

Dick's Bar

192 2nd Avenue @ 2th Street, Manhattan
Everyday 2pm-4am, 212.475.2071

Dick's has withstood the onslaught of hipsterism that has infiltrated this once shady part of town, reflecting a grittier, no bullshit East Village of days gone by. The dreary red and black color scheme makes it seem even darker and smokier here than it actually is. Adding to the look are a couple of video poker machines near the door, a shopping cart hanging on the wall, a spinning wig atop an out-of-commission telephone booth, and random pictures of gas tanks. Drink specials are listed on an old sandwich board. There's a pool table, almost always in use later at night, in a cramped back area. Everything's a bit off kilter, and that makes for a good place to write or ruminate.

The jukebox has a great selection of obscure late 70's/early 80's new wave and punk, but it isn't always in use. From 4pm to 9pm there's a happy hour which gets you a dollar or two off most drinks, and there are varied specials list for the rest of the night. In general, Dick's is cheap relative to the surrounding area. Monday is show tune night, and on Tuesday and Thursday they show old porn. Older regulars populate the place from early afternoon until the wee hours of the morning, along with random locals, bar hoppers, gaggles of friends looking for a place to chat, and loners looking to be alone.

Dick's is the perfect warm-up spot for a raunchy night at the Cock, which is two avenues east, and is also around the corner from the livelier Phoenix. If you need to drink alone and heavily in the East Village, Dick's Bar is your best bet.

Your Words: "What a bar should be — cheap drinks and friendly folks." "I come here with my boyfriend to chill."

Dugout

185 Christopher Street @ Weehawken Street, Manhattan
Everyday 4pm-4am, 212.242.9113

Every city has its bear bar. San Francisco has the Lone Eagle, Toronto has Tool Box, and in New York The Dugout is the place for bears to be. At the west end of Christopher Street, The Dugout looks like a neighborhood frat bar, with neon beer signs, paneled walls, a cigarette machine in back, a pool table in front, and that's pretty much it, except for the Metrobear Patrol sign. It's the perfect setting for the unpretentious men that kick back here.

If you're an admirer of bears, Sunday Beer Blast at the Dugout is beyond heavenly. If you feel stifled by body-obsessed boys talking about nutritional supplements and bench presses at other bars, the Dugout could be your beer-soaked home away from home. From 1pm to 10pm, there are more deliciously hairy chests and luscious round bellies than you can shake your stick at. Friends come with friends, but there are single men with roving eyes also. The $2.50 drafts keep smiles on everyone's bearded faces. If it's so packed you can't breathe, chill outside the bar on the sidewalk near the Pier, and hang out with a gregarious, fun bunch.

> **"You're born naked, and the rest is drag."**
>
> **RUPAUL**

The rest of the week isn't quite as eventful, but draws a sizable laid-back crowd of all ages most nights. The music from the jukebox is usually predictable pop, though you're more likely to hear "Sweet Home Alabama" or Guns N' Roses here than at other places. Mixed drinks prices tend to run a bit high, but this is a place to do a shot and down a Bud. Ever feel like you want to take your shirt off at a club but you haven't been in a gym since high school? Come to the Dugout and let loose.

Your Words: "Sunday is sweaty, friendly, really hot." "What a gay bar should be — a place to feel comfortable in your own skin."

Eight of Clubs

250 W 75th Street @ Broadway, Manhattan
M-Tu 4pm-4am, W-Su noon-4am, 212.580.7389

Nobody at the Eight of Clubs seems to remember just how long this gem of a place has been around. This might be because they've all been taking advantage of the $3 beer specials. This discreet below-street level bar sports a jukebox featuring old show tunes, jazz classics, rock, soul and beyond. The crowd reflects the same healthy mix.

Queers of all ages, races, and social backgrounds are chilling out, relaxing, talking shit, picking each other up, and what-have-you under the dim lights.

The walls are adorned with headshots of movie stars, with Al Pacino, Mae West and everyone in between putting in a cameo. But don't be fooled into thinking that the Eight of Clubs is any kind of novelty joint — the vibe can be downright seductive. The backyard garden area seems to be entirely made of dark corners, and serves as a great place for a romantic encounter, or to just forget you're in the city and stargaze for a while. The bartenders are conversational and friendly, and genuinely care about the customers. They're the kind of bartenders who will warn you about a psycho, or call you a taxi if you've drank too much. You get the impression they'd probably be hanging out there even if they weren't getting paid.

There are plenty of happy hour specials, but prices are always reasonable. The early afternoon hours Wednesday through Sunday are convenient for people who work the night shift, or clubgoers who need to take the rough edges off the previous night's festivities. Smack in the heart of the Upper West Side, Eight of Clubs is a perfect place for locals, and also worth a subway trip.

Your Words: "I come after work for a drink, and end up staying all night." "The drinks are dirt cheap, the bartenders are great, and there's a real sense of community here."

Fat Cock 29

29 2nd Avenue @ 2nd Street, Manhattan
Everyday 5pm-4am, 212.946.1871

The younger, gentler sibling to the infamous Cock, FC29 is a haven for 80's aficionados. You can play Asteroids and Galaga while the DJ spins Olivia Newton-John's Greatest Hits, or munch Doritos at the bar while your friend sifts through Adam Ant and George Michael CDs at the jukebox. Like the delirious decade, FC29 is punky, fun and saturated in color.

The main attraction is the huge video projection at the end of the bar. Whoever splices together the kitschy, horny random images they show nightly is a true artist. The crowds gawk and chuckle at montages of whirring Wonder Woman conversions, which lead into 70s porn clips, which lead into Soul Train line dancers. Watching 70s porn on a life-size screen is an experience in itself. The video serves as an entertaining distraction if you're alone, or a conversation piece if you're hooking up. The bar is 20-odd stools long, and necks are always craned to the video action.

Tarzan's Load, Pucker Up Tight Ass, and Fizz Jizz are just a sample of the specialty drinks listed on FC29's blackboard. Drinks are somewhat expensive but always potent. The bartenders chew the fat with the regulars and are attentive to newcomers. During the week the crowds can be sparse, but on the weekends it's cramped with mostly local, fashion-conscious Village boys. Large, cushy couches line the walls, and groups of friends/co-workers/gym buddies often meet here and whoop it up.

For gay boys with short attention spans, Fat Cock 29 is minutes away from The Bar and The Boiler Room, and conveniently a couple blocks from the F train. For fellows who want to settle down for the night in a welcoming yet trashy atmosphere and drink themselves silly, FC29 is also perfect.

Your Words: "I sat, drank, and stared at the screen for two hours. I could've done that at home, but it's more fun here." "FC29 takes me back. It feels like a freshman college party."

Friend's Tavern

"There is always room for friends" is written across the top of the bar at Friend's Tavern and on their business card. Ironically, the place gets so crowded on weekends there's barely any room for friends or anyone else. Not quite as friendly as the Music Box down the street, Friend's is a great place to meet Queens guys, drink yourself silly during Happy Hour, and then shake it off on the small dance floor in the back.

The place has personality. Paper decorations hang from the ceiling as well as hundreds of Christmas lights. The crowd is young, hip and cute and nightly DJs keep them moving. There are drink specials throughout the week, including concoctions all night Wednesday, half price domestic beers on Friday until 8pm, and specially priced drinks from 10pm to 2am on Sundays. Willie the Bartender is back, and manning happy hour 4pm to 8pm daily. A mean-looking bouncer mans the door on weekends, and will throw your ass out if you're causing any trouble. Special events are held throughout the year including holiday parties and a candle light feast, and drag performers strut their stuff on selected nights throughout the year.

Bartenders are experienced and amiable. Their pictures are featured on friendstavern.com if you want to check them out in advance! Also on their website is a message board where one can leave a message to friends to meet them at Friend's, and a complete listing of specials, parties, and featured DJs. If you want to get your groove on and drink cheaply, you can't go wrong at Friend's.

Your Words: "Where all my buddies go in Queens." "The only gay place to dance in Jackson Heights."

G

225 W 19th Street, Manhattan, Everyday 4pm-4am, 212.929.1085

G has the reputation of being trendy to a fault, conjuring stereotyped images of plastic Chelsea boys drinking fruity drinks in a fruity setting. While the staff can seem a bit detached and the air a little chilly, it is possible to have good old-fashioned fun with friends here or meet a well-to-do stranger. The front and back rooms have plenty of places to sit, and are always full of chatty Kathies. Lots of them reside within a ten-block radius, but uptowners, out-of-towners, students and bridge-and-tunnel thrill seekers descend upon the legend that is G. They line up outside on weekends, and take advantage of half-price happy hours.

The centerpiece of G is the oval bar in the center of the space, stylishly lit from the inside. Circling the bar are boys standing, posing and throwing furtive glances around the room. They have a good view of each other as well as loungers in the other rooms. Sometimes couples will slink away from the action in the adjacent narrow nook with tiny tables and three pay phones (even though everyone's on their cell). DJs spin every night and the music and sound system are club-worthy, making G a good place to meet friends before heading to one of the nearby clubs. Drinks are on the pricey side, and the bartenders are way too busy to make small talk.

G is glamorous, conservative, upscale, minimalist and pretty. It is the bar version of the overflowing Big Cup café around the corner. If a fashion model reincarnated as a bar, he would be G. Put on your best Banana shirt, and cast dispersions.

Your Words: "An antidote to the grungy dives you usually encounter in the gay world." "I go and pretend I'm someone else."

Ginger's Bar

363 5th Avenue, Between 5th & 6th Avenues, Park Slope, Brooklyn
Nightly until 4am, 718.788.0924

Ginger's is one of the best bars, queer or otherwise, in New York. On a quiet street in trendy Park Slope, it's worth a trip from Manhattan. Everything about the space puts a stranger at ease — the rustic décor, smiling customers, amiable bartenders, and a great beer selection.

The glass window at the entrance is lined with quaint, unrelated knick-knacks. A red fire alarm sits above ceramic clogs from Holland, which sit above faded photographs and letters. The front room is long and regal. Tables line the left, and the bar, adorned with beer steins and stained glass, takes up the right side. The back room is reminiscent of an English pub. There are many small tables and benches, a red velvet pool table and a dart board. Pictures of musicians hang on the walls, and a rocking horse hangs from the ceiling. There are lots of places for conversation.

An accordion sits on top of the jukebox, which contains a solid mix of old and new pop and soul, from Booker T & the MGs to Deee-lite. The sound system is good and the music isn't too loud. The clientele is predominantly lesbian, but lots of locals, male and female, straight and gay, come around. Friday and Saturday nights are packed, and there's usually a small crowd during the week.

Ginger's has 10 beers on tap, and quite a selection at that, including Stella Artois, Boddington's, and RamRod. The bartenders are more than friendly, giving hugs to locals as they walk in the door. The customers are just as gregarious, offering to play a song on the jukebox if you're waiting in line, or starting up a game of darts.

Formerly the popular Carry Nation, Ginger's has been flourishing for a year, down the street from another worthy gay bar, Excelsior. As sociable as an English pub and as comfortable as your living room, Ginger's is great any night of the week.

Your Words: "I feel like I'm in the South when I'm here. Everybody's so nice." "...a spot for romance."

Halcyon

227 Smith Street @ Butler Street, Carroll Gardens, Brooklyn
S-Th 10am-midnight, F-Sa 10am-2am, 718.260.9299
www.halcyonline.com

Halcyon is the future of the community café. The design is unique but not pretentious, the DJs out of this world, and the atmosphere stylish but not off-putting. Customers sit at 50's dinette set and marvel at the collection of old, colorful anachronisms sitting on shelves along the wall: thrift store paintings, framed crochet creations, cocktail shakers, airline shoulder bags, and much more. It looks like a swinging singles pad exploded. Pick up some Barnum Animal Crackers at the counter, or order from a wide drink selection — Young's Oatmeal Stout, Original Sin Hard Cider or some Framboise. Citysearch.com voted Halcyon the Best Coffee Bar this past year and the baristas can indeed whip up whatever you want.

Halcyon sells vinyl in the back, and whoever buys for the store knows their shit. The classifications aren't as simple as house, techno, etc. Choose from Global Beats, Frisco Disco, or Wave Music sections. The talented DJs take their cue from the store (or maybe vice versa) and spin a wide variety of music. On different nights Tech House, bossa influenced new jazz, two step garage, experimental dub, etc. No dancing, but the DJs are so good you want to stand near the speakers and marvel at the sounds.

The crowd is mixed. Whenever quality music is playing, both gay and straight beatmongers will show up. Lesbian couples, self-conscious scenesters, and kids from around the area will chill in the garden outside or rummage through the vinyl. Everyone feels comfortable. Forget Manhattan — Halcyon is the place to be.

Your Words: "I learn a lot about new music just by hanging out here." "I shouldn't have to hang out with just straight people or just gay people. Halcyon brings everything together."

Hangar Bar

115 Christopher Street @ Bleecker Street, Manhattan
M-Th 3pm-4am, F-Su 2pm-4am, 212.627.2044

One of the newest kids on the block, the Hangar has carved a distinctive niche on a street with no shortage of old reliable queer watering holes. It's popular with Village residents, Chelsea boys and tourists from all over, and everyone's made to feel welcome.

The window at the entrance offers a fish-eye view of Christopher Street, and boys perch on stools and watch the passerbys. There are two bars — the main one that travels far from front to back, and a smaller, cozier one behind the pool table in the rear. Happy hour is from 3pm to 9pm Monday through Friday and all day Tuesday is always packed, partially because of cute and kind bartender Steve, who's been around since Hangar opened eight years ago. Munchies are provided (pigs-in-the-blanket even!) and the music varies — the staff is really knowledgeable and will occasionally play mix CDs brought in by customers. Classics, house, rock — whatever

> "If my mother was responsible for it, I am grateful."
>
> **CHRISTOPHER ISHERWOOD**

the mood is that day.

Nights can be insanely cruisy. The easy going crowd is impossible to pigeonhole — boys of all races of all ages hang out here at all times. So at 2am when carousers haven't found the love of their life or the lust of their night yet, Hangar is a good destination for lots of different guys. The affability of the staff affects the crowd, creating an atmosphere for getting to know each other. There are cool DJs on the weekend also, and bartenders are quick and efficient. Beer Blast on Sunday is always popular. Whether starting or finishing a night in the West Village, Hangar Bar is perfect.

Your Words: "A straightforward, no-attitude kind of place. Bartenders are sweet." "The addition of the bar in the back makes it nicer."

Hannah's Lava Lounge

923 8th Avenue, Between 54th & 55th Streets, Manhattan
Everyday noon-4am, 212.974.9087

Hidden amidst the shady porn shops and prostitutes of Eighth Avenue lies one of New York City's best kept secrets. Under a large, white "Westerly Liquor" sign, only a small etching of the bar's name on the window indicates that it even exists. Hailed by New York Magazine as NYC's best gay dive, Hannah's has all the cozy qualities of a neighborhood bar. The bartender knows your drink and everybody knows your name. The bar is small, clean, worn and scarred. Lighting is limited to lava lamps, and fluorescent love beads line the entrance. The artwork of unknown gay NYC artists is displayed and renewed monthly.

Lacking the pomp and circumstance of most gay bars, Hannah's Lava Lounge counters the typical cruise-fest mentality of some bars with a homey and accepting atmosphere. At any given time, the bar will be lined with people from all walks of life; theater patrons, drag queens, gym boys and lesbians are just a section of this community of regulars who mix and mingle with anybody in search of good conversation. The enthusiastic and attentive bar staff includes a social worker, an up-and-coming actor and a champion barrel racer on the gay rodeo circuit.

Through fundraisers, Sunday bingo, Thursday drag shows and occasional all night happy hours, Hannah's keeps the midtown crowd coming back. Instead of a night with techno, expensive drinks, drama and facades, dress how you like, be who you are, and belly up to this quaint little bar where they're always willing to welcome another queer into their ever-growing family.

Your Words: "A pleasant, comfortable and eclectic group of somebody's." "Get down on it! Hannah's is groovy."

Hell

59 Gansevoort Street @ Washington Street, Manhattan
Sa-Th 7pm-4am, F 5pm-4am, 212.727.1666

Timotheo, jovial bartender at Hell, describes his place of employment as "the lobby to the gates of Hell." If only Satan's domain were this attractive. While lots of bars in the Village are a bit tattered around the edges, Hell is a sublime, swank lounge in the middle of the grungy meatpacking district.

Hell is red — red lights, red walls, and red velvet curtains. The walls are covered with

hundreds of celebrity headshots — all with devil horns on their pretty heads. Tony Orlando, the Partridge Family, Jimmie Walker — they're all going to hell. If drunk, spend some time looking at the photos, reminiscing and laughing your ass off. There are comfy couches to sprawl out on in the back, and tables and stools throughout the decently large space. Drinks are expensive and generally worth the price. In a glass lined with cinnamon, the pear martini is delicious. Cosmopolitans are awesome. Razz Rum Rita, a raspberry daiquiri, goes down smoothly also. They also offer coffee drinks — Mexican, Irish, Roman, etc. Other drinks' names include Fallen Angel and Wicked Bitch.

The crowd is mixed straight and gay, about 25% female, young, attractive and laid back. The jukebox selection fits the surroundings. Most of the selections lie on the hipper side of pop — Massive Attack, Soul II Soul, and lots of 80s stuff. DJs on Tuesday, Wednesday and Thursday spin an eclectic mix and generally play to the crowd.

Open 4 years ago by the owner of Chelsea's fabulous Big Cup, Hell adds a welcome twist to the old school mix of West Village gay bars. For a schizophrenic evening, after a visit to Hell go to the raunchy Lure around the corner after sipping on martinis.

Your Words: "This is a good place to bring anybody — relatives, friends, whatever." "Pretty classy — you would never know from the outside."

Henrietta Hudson

438 Hudson Street @ Morton Street, Manhattan
Everyday 8pm-5am, 212.924.3347

In 2001, Henrietta Hudson celebrated their ten-year anniversary, an eternity by NYC standards. The endurance of the club is an indication of its ability to appease an often ambivalent city crowd. Owner Lisa Cannistraci, who has been in the biz for over twenty years, knows exactly what it takes to keep her gay sisters and brothers coming back for more.

If you ask the patrons what it is that brings them back to HH, a few might say Susan Morabito, an occasional guest DJ known throughout the gay circuit, or superstar DJ Merritt, who spins an eclectic mix of soulful house every Friday night. Another group might insist that the Sunday night dyke band fest is a must see. And still others will tell you that the drink prices ($4-9) and small cover ($5) allow them to return without causing a major dent in their finances. However, what almost all these customers will tell you is that the staff is the most appealing aspect of Henrietta Hudson. This pleasant mix of bouncers, bartenders and managers engage, entertain and please their clientele from the moment the door opens until they close the doors in the early morning. While the staff has their own vocations, ranging from photographer and animal rescue to private investigator, they treat this second job as a vacation. They enjoy the nights as much as their patrons.

Although known as a lesbian bar, the crowd is very mixed and cruisy, especially during the "Boy+Girl=Fun" party on Wednesday nights. Lotsa boys and even more girls dance the night away on the small dance floor in the front room, while the fairly new sideroom and bar offers an opportunity to lounge, converse or play a game of pool. The age range may run anywhere from 21-40, but the crowd in general steers toward youth. In any case, the group is sexy, beautiful and very relaxed. HH is set up in every way to make fun the only possibility.

Owner Lisa Cannistraci is known for her witty euphemisms and her appreciation for a good shoe. On any night, a luxurious loafer can gain you free admittance into a place she dubs as one "where you can feel comfortable in your own skin...or someone else's."

Your Words: "Diverse, obviously fun and undeniably sexual — all that you could expect of a dance club." "It may be the one lesbian bar where everyone feels comfortable."

Julie's

305 E 53rd Street @ First Avenue, Manhattan
W-Sa 8pm-4am, 212.688.1294

Have you ever heard the song "Julie's Blanket" by Mary's Danish? They're a great band, and that song should always remind you of this place. But anyway.

Julie's flyers say "Something For the Ladies," their drink specials apply to "Ladies Only," and they're not being ironic. The space attracts more ladies than, say, riot grrrls or Dykes on Bikes. To attract a younger crowd, what used to be an upscale piano bar has now been converted into a fresher space with a small dance floor. Some like the new space better; some like the old. Some diss the new space by saying it looks like a hotel bar. What's wrong with hotel bars? There's always a smattering of casual clubgoers here, but the crowd as a whole knows how to dress for a night out. The mix changes slightly night by night depending on what the DJ is spinning; Monday is R&B, Wednesday salsa & merengue cause hips to shake, and Friday house and reggae gets the ladies moving.

A proper and tactful essence pervades the room at Julie's. The women love their music and sway to the sounds with a sensual synchronicity, but the dancers aren't overtly sexual. The Friday night go-go girls woo the crowd with elegance and beauty. No raunch is required.

> "Heterosexuality is not normal, it's just common."
>
> **DOROTHY PARKER**

The Dark Room, the club's back lounge area, seems to be one big slumber party, filled with conversation and laughter, unlike the desperate feel of most NYC "backrooms." The attentive, cute and courteous staff supplies the ladies of the evening with reasonably priced drinks ($4-$8) and genuine smiles. There's often a smattering of men, but mostly only women kick back here. Like most East Side bars, Julie's attracts a fair number of loyal regulars, and some visitors staying nearby. Wherever you're from, Julie's makes for a pleasant night out.

Your Words: "Julie's is comfy, civilized and a nice place to hang after work." "I come here for the people. We're a close-knit group that knows how to have fun."

Julius'

159 W 10th Street @ Waverly Place, Manhattan
M-Sa 8pm-4am, Su noon-3am, 212.929.9672

One of the oldest operating bars in New York City, Julius' is rich in history and culture. Hundreds of autographed pictures of 20th century greats cover the walls, from Lena Horne to Jack Dempsey to a 1941 Chicago Bears team photo signed by George Salas. How many gay bars have a testimonial from Walter Winchell hanging in their back room? Julius' opened in 1862, and has been gay since the 1940's. Tennessee Williams and the members of the pioneering Mattachine society used to imbibe here back in the day, and hallmark queen film Boys in the Band was shot here.

Today the mostly 40+ locals chat with the experienced bartenders at the old wooden bar, gather at the many tables in the back, or look out the huge windows at the Christopher Street crowd. Across from the bar oddly enough is a mini-kitchen, famous for it's big, juicy burgers. The jukebox plays all the divas, but some unexpected CDs like Artie Shaw and the Animals are included in the mix. There's a television at the bar, which often plays Wheel of Fortune for some reason. Drinks are pretty strong and moderately priced.

Julius' gets most crowded Thursdays and Fridays from 4pm to 8pm for happy hour, and is loosely populated at other times. It's a great place to start out a Village pub-crawl, whether popping in and out of gay watering holes, or checking out some other historical bars in the area such as White Horse Tavern on Hudson Ave. and Chumley's on Bedford St. While Stonewall is a must stop on any gay history jaunt, so is Julius'.

Your Words: "Away from the rat race." "Quiet and comfortable." "You can always find good conversation here."

The Lure

409 W 13th Street, Between Washington Street & 9th Avenue, Manhattan, M-Sa 8pm-4am, 212.741.3919, www.thelure.com

Where have all the leather bars gone? It's like they all packed up and relocated to San Francisco. Long standing leather bars The Eagle and Spike have closed after decades of serving the chaps and cock ring crowd.

Thankfully, The Lure makes up for the lack of leather in this town. The space is cavernous. Huge cages sit ominously in the far corner in the main room, along with large hanging drawings of penises, a Harley Davidson pinball machine, and a bench press. In the adjacent room, guys sit on long bleachers and watch porno. Nearby, someone's checking out someone else's privates in the bathroom.

The freaks come out for Pork on Wednesdays. The muscles and sweat will have you salivating. You can also send pix on the website for the Pork Porn model search. Thursdays bring the Chubb Club, and Friday and Saturday are leather only. Foot Friends meet on Wednesday, and The Renegades, a religious leather club, meets here often.

> "It doesn't matter what you wear, they're checking out your savoir-faire."
>
> **RUPAUL**

This may be the only club in New York where special nights don't include drag queens. The guys here are rough, or at least look rough. The DJs are hot, spin a variety of stuff, and their pictures are on the website.

The Lure is unlike any other bar in New York. Not for the faint of heart, it can be intimidating when you first walk in. But if leather and flesh is your thing, slide on your armband and check The Lure out.

Your Words: "I get a boner just thinking about that place. Drinks at the Lure and an hour at J's, and I'm good for the week." "An antidote to the foofiness pervading the rest of the city."

The Monster

80 Grove Street near 7th Avenue, Manhattan
Everyday 4pm-4am, 212.924.3558

The upstairs piano bar area at The Monster is the closest thing to a gay TGIFriday's that you'll ever see. It's packed, it's loud, and for some reason everyone seems to be having the time of their lives. You'll be shocked to see such a huge, lively crowd on a gray Wednesday afternoon. It'll take a good five minutes to squeeze close enough to the bar to get one of their tasty margaritas ($6.25). After your drink, settle for standing by one of their huge windows looking out onto Christopher Street, instead of unsuccessfully looking for a seat. There's a diverse crowd here, from the bridge and tunnel crowd to locals, from older queers to barely legal cuties. People seemed downright giddy to spend some time with their significant other. So giddy in fact that there are copious amounts of PDAs here. From the lengthy smooch to the shameless ass-grab, the art of subtlety is completely lost here. The sizable bar has enough room for a grand piano, which crooners crowd around. The group belts out showtunes in their huskiest voices, some of them taking it quite seriously. The hotel-quality framed paintings on the wall complement the soft color scheme and numerous vases of fresh flowers sprinkled throughout the space.

When the sun goes down, the downstairs opens up. The Monster may be the best place in New York for dancing your ass off while paying little to get in. For a small cover, gyrate to house and dance hits. Sometimes the atmosphere is so positive down here that it feels like a house party — people swap dance partners and talk to each other without being overtly sexual or cruisy.

The Monster's been around forever, and for good reason. The combination of piano bar and dance club is strange, but it works. For a night of frolicking and fun in the West Village, go to Stonewall, pay homage to your ancestors; then go to the Monster and pay homage to Stephen Sondheim and Ultra Nate.

Your Words: "Oh honey, I'm so happy to see you!" "Dancing without the attitude or huge cover."

The Music Box

40-08 74th Street, Jackson Heights, Queens
Everyday 4pm-4am, 718.429.9356

Step off the Roosevelt Ave. subway stop in Jackson Heights and walk right into The Music Box. It's kind of hidden next to a Japanese restaurant on 74th St., but there's a strange looking iguana on the green awning, and at night you can see the DJ working hard through the front window. Above the front corner of the bar, a ceramic Virgin Mary casts a holy glow on the proceedings. Look down the bar and you'll see a mostly Latin crowd laughing and talking. Everyone's hugging each other hello or goodbye, saying Hi on the way to the bathroom, or introducing someone to a friend.

The space is long and narrow with the wooden bar stretching 2/3 of the way down. Opposite the bar are lots of tables and seats. There's a pool table in the back with a bench next to it for an audience. DJs spin Latin house, gay dance tracks, salsa and soca on the weekends, and on the weekends the jukebox blasts Latin and pop favorites. Happy hour is from 4pm to 8pm during the week and draws a decent crowd. Weekends are busy but thankfully not packed to the hilt. The crowd is handsome and young, mostly male with frequent female friends on the weekends. The bartenders are quick and polite.

The Music Box feels like someone's house party — close quarters, guys joking around, and generally a warm atmosphere. If you need to get away from your usual Manhattan haunts for a while, The Music Box is a good choice on the weekends. If you live in the area, definitely check it out.

Your Words: "I take friends there on Saturday's sometimes. There's no attitude." "A good, homey, easy-going bar."

Ninth Avenue Saloon

656 9th Avenue @ 46th Street, Manhattan
Everyday 8am-4am, 212.307.1503

This friendly dive bar on the busy 9th Ave. strip has a lot going for it. To your right when you walk in are three shelves of random books from Robert Parker to Betty Friedan. It's a lending library for customers. Below it is a basket of condoms. How many bars give away condoms anymore? Ninth Avenue Saloon treats its customers well in many ways.

Bartender Jesse works the nightshift and will crack you up. He does a drag show once every month. Drinks are cheap relative to the area — get your beer on tap for only $2.50. On Sunday, 50 cents from each drink benefits God's Love We Deliver. Munch on popcorn from the old fashioned popper behind the bar. Regulars, mostly in their 30s and 40s, are social rather than cliquey. A common crowd: A lei artist from Hawaii, a man with little to no short-term memory, and a weatherman. A theatergoing crowd also filters in some nights, and who knows what you'll find here when they open at 8am.

The jukebox at the Saloon is a new-fangled contraption called Touch Tone. Put your dollar in, point to a song on the screen and it plays. Beware: Your Toni Tony Tone selection may interrupt "If you get drunk in New York City" coming from the stereo behind the bar. But, nobody will make a fuss.

Weird jukebox + weird people + cheap drinks + animated bartenders + lending library = a great personality for an unassuming little bar in Hell's Kitchen.

Your Words: "This place attracts a more laid back crowd than other places in Midtown." "Thank God there are still cool places to hang out near Times Square."

Oscar Wilde

221 E 58th Street @ Second Avenue, Manhattan
Nightly until 4am, 212.489.7309

The importance of being fun is a priority for everyone at Oscar Wilde, an unassuming bar on the East Side. Despite the area and its pol- ished ambiance, Wilde has no dress code and a reassuringly relaxed manner that sets it apart from its Midtown neighbors.

The incredibly long bar to the left, not alone in its claim to be the city's longest, stretches from one end of the narrow room to the other. Everyone from businessmen to the destitute perch on stools at the bar, and there's a small space toward the back for a few couches. The insanely long happy hour runs all week from 4pm to 10pm. The most expensive martini is only six bucks, and one of the seven beers on tap goes for just $3 a pint. The commitment to affordable drunkenness is cemented by the $2 Bloody Mary Sunday.

The décor is rather unremarkable, but Wilde gains its notoriety from its music. The jukebox, reaching near legendary status in the city, is miraculously updated weekly and contains a diverse selection. Around 10pm with the after-work crowd gone, the lights go down, the music goes up, and the disco ball starts spinning. It's a young and friendly crowd that keeps the party alive and kicking until the wee hours.

Wilde can get pretty cruisy late night, but the atmosphere still feels relaxed and unpressured. The signs in the bathroom asking for only one patron in the stall at a time reads as part-warning/part-challenge. With the music pumping and no attitude to contend with, it's hard not to let your hair down and have a good time here.

Your Words: "Everybody knows everybody here. There's always a good time to be had."

Pegasus Bar

119 E 60th Street, Between Lexington & Park Avenues, Manhattan
Nightly until 4am, 212.888.4702

Amidst the gaudy showmanship beaming from the enormous windows of the area's high-end department stores stands the reclusive Pegasus Bar, nestled on the lower fringe of the Upper East Side. Step inside past the frosted glass etching of the bar's namesake, and you'll be surprised to find an inviting and intimate neighborhood bar.

The front room, complete with an elegant black piano played Wednesday through Saturday, accommodates a loyal after-work following. Three-piece suits mingle with jeans, discussing anything from politics to sex to the affected artwork adorning the walls (the artist changes every month). The small bar serves bottled beer and mixed drinks for a pricey four bucks and up, which would be a problem if the bartenders weren't so pleasant. They control the music as well as the frequent informal drink specials. Consider yourself lucky if you get to try Junior's Chi Pirinha, a Brazilian concoction of crushed limes, sugar, and a whole lot of rum for only $3.50.

As the night goes on, Pegasus sheds its more refined edges as a younger, more diverse crowd shuffles in. Thursday, Friday and Saturday are the best nights to frolic here, when the more playful backroom opens up. With plastic-wrapped leopard skin benches, a separate bar, and a small but effective stereo system, this place can rock. The centerpiece is the small stage, hosting the occasional play or feisty cabaret show, but mostly karaoke over the weekend. The crowd mix becomes mostly Asian, and customers croon in various languages.

> "Sick and perverted always appeals to me."
>
> **MADONNA**

Although Pegasus is host to its share of nightly love connections, the atmosphere is less racy and more congenial. There are business cards at the bar that leave room for a name, number and email in case you get lucky. Pegasus Bar is great place to feel comfortable among friendly folk, relax, or sing your heart out.

Your Words: "Everybody talks to everybody. It's pretty hard not to feel comfortable." "One of the few places on the Upper East Side where I can be myself."

Phoenix

447 E 13th Street @ Avenue A, Manhattan
Everyday 4pm-4am, 212.477.9979

Quirky and comfortable, Phoenix is a popular destination for East Village dwellers. It has the right mix of sociability and seediness to appease the hardcore barfly as well as wide-eyed newcomers. The bartenders are Prozac-friendly, engaging the boys in conversation, recognizing repeat customers, and treating regulars like family. They're partially why the place is always busy from open to close.

Another reason is the jukebox. Where else can you find Southern Culture on the Skids, the Orb, X, the new Madonna single, the Pixies, a Soul Train 1971 collection, and a compilation called Fistfuckers In the Hot Tub? With lots of competition, it may be the best jukebox in the East Village. Be patient though — guys will stand there making their decisions for hours, and you may have to wait a while before your songs are played. Adding to the entertainment is a Ms. Pacman/Galaga video game, almost as addicting as the jukebox, and a pool table almost always in use in the back.

Phoenix gets cruisy, especially late at night, but it's more of a place for flirting and mingling. Nice boys hang out here, and happy hour from 4pm to 8pm brings a few females into the mix, many of them avid pool players. There a cozy side room for chatting complete with sofas, chairs and plants. How do plants cope with the smoke? Drink prices are normal for the area, and there are frequent specials throughout the week. A great place to hang out before heading 50 paces over to the down and dirty Cock, Phoenix is a reliable watering hole any day of the week.

Your Words: "I've been coming here for years." "The bar staff here is really special. They love each other and all the customers."

Pieces

8 Christopher Street @ Greenwich Avenue, Manhattan
Everyday 2pm-4am, 212.929.9291

On its website, Pieces claims "It's not just a bar… it's a party!" They're not kidding. With nightly events, long happy hours, dancing bartenders, silly videos, and one of the best karaoke nights in the city, this bar can make you giddy with happiness.

The décor is cheesy, like some trashy midwestern gay couple converted their basement into a gay bar. The bright neon lit P-I-E-C-E-S glimmering in the Christopher St. window is shadowed by long-ass 70's beads. Clips of Grease 2, West Side Story and Lucy are playing while some crusty Diana King or Whitney Houston hit booms out a pretty amazing sound system. The stage is covered with silver fringe, and around the holidays you're bound to see paper decorations similar to the ones used during your elementary school years. And there are not one, but three disco balls. There is no pretension here.

Let the staff of Pieces entertain you. Lucky Thursdays brings Personals Post Office where each customer gets his own "address" and hopefully "mail" from an admirer. From Saturday through Monday, order a Long Island Iced Tea for $3 and get trashed very quickly. Throughout the week there are live shows, drag impressions, and original drink specials.

Nothing beats Tuesday's Karaoke though. They've been doing it eight years, and it shows. The hosts warm the crowd up by singing a couple of songs, and truly make everyone feel at home. A few of the performances make a child want to cry, but you would never know it by the audience reaction. The supportive atmosphere makes up for every shred of attitude ever experienced inside the walls of gay bars. At one point, every single person in the bar bellowed the Golden Girls "Thank you for being a friend" theme song, almost bringing tears to some. You can also actually burn your star performance on a CD.

Never a cover charge and always something going on, Pieces has become a safe haven for locals and tourists alike.

Your Words: "This place is completely ludicrous. I come here all the time." "My boyfriend loves it. I can't keep him away."

Posh

405 W 51st Street @ 9th Avenue, Manhattan
Everyday 4pm-4am, 212.957.2222

Back in the day when Jack didn't trade barbs with Karen and rimming in Pittsburgh wasn't a main attraction on cable television, the exterior of a gay bar didn't draw attention to itself who didn't want to be seen going into such a place. Windows were blacked out, and signs were small or nonexistent. Posh's outside seating demonstrates how far we as a people have come! Gay boys and girls getting trashed on the sidewalk for all the world to see is an overdue occurrence.

It's not all that posh, but this stately little bar in Hell's Kitchen, the neighborhood most likely to be the next Chelsea, is a welcome addition to the burgeoning scene. A sheer curtain separates the sleek bar from the cozy back room. Like the View Bar in Chelsea, the open exterior of Posh attracts passersby — straight couples wandering in from busy Ninth Avenue shoot the breeze with down-to-earth queer locals. Type-A personalities try to pick up the hot, straight bartenders, so hooking up isn't out of the question. Jason the Bartender is especially attractive, makes the drinks strong, and works his ass off.

Different nights attract different crowds. Saturday is Bare Ass and Leather Night with $2.50 beer specials, while Wednesday is Torrey's Cosmo Night. Posh is new and still trying to find its niche, but sometimes that's the best time to go to a bar — when the atmosphere is more fresh and less been-there-done-that.

Your Words: "It reminds me of a quiet Chelsea bar." "The mood is different every night." "A good place for a drink after Restaurant Row dining."

Rawhide

212 8th Avenue @ 21st Street, Manhattan
M-Sa 8am-4am, Su noon-4am, 212.242.9332

First of all, if you're looking for the perfect cheap gift to buy a person who already has everything and needs nothing, buy him a Rawhide coffee mug for five bucks. All his other mugs will pale in comparison. The ashtray is also perfect for smokers at three bucks, and a Rawhide stuffed bear is a cute subversive trinket for that niece who won't shut up. If not, shop for one of the moustached men leaning against a post. They are ready for you.

In contrast to the post-modern foofiness of the newer Chelsea bars, Rawhide is down, dirty — the real deal. The night crowd is comprised of 40 and 50 year-old leather daddies, beer-bellied bears, and guys that have been around the block a few hundred times. The bartenders are tough but kind, handsome and look like they walked out of the Tom of Finland drawings hanging on the walls. A sign behind the bar reads "It is illegal to argue with the bartender" — your ass will hit the pavement if

> "When you asked for a date, I thought you were straight. Johnny are you queer?"
>
> **JOSIE COTTON**

you act up. This bar isn't messing around. Half of the bar is fenced in by wooden poles and benches, and guys sit and stand close to each other. They are not shy. The younger after-after-hours set rolls in at 8am. Partiers coming down from whatever drug they did and worn-out boys from the sex spots around town end up here. The blackened windows thankfully keep out the light.

Rawhide feels like a San Francisco watering hole, even though it's smack in the middle of Chelseaville. You could almost smell the poppers from days gone by. It's not strictly a leather bar, but you wouldn't feel out of place in chaps.

Your Words: "Growl." "The black hole of Chelsea."

Regents

317 E 53rd Street @ 2nd Avenue, Manhattan
Restaurant: Everyday 4pm-11pm, Bar: Su-Th 7pm-1am,
F-Sa 7pm-2am, 212.593.3091

Regents has the perfect combination bar/restaurant for the older, more moneyed gentleman of NYC. The restaurant features primarily American cuisine, ranging from their famous Homestyle Meatloaf to Beer Battered Fish and Chips. This "meat and potato" joint prides itself on its hefty portions at reasonable prices, which range from $12.95-18.95. To add a little zest and zing to the static menu, Regents also offers five rotating specials as well as a $17.95 Prix Fixe menu offering a choice of soup, salad, or appetizer as well as an entree. Drinks prices are moderate, range from $5-7.

While the dining room is spacious and conducive to a quiet and uninterrupted dining experience, the piano bar has both an intimate and communal decorative style. Plush couches, lounge chairs and settees, envelop a small central bar; framed and signed Playbills align all the walls. A faux marble fireplace emits cozy light in a room already bright with enthusiasm and good, old-fashioned fun. A nightly cabaret featuring an open mike begins nightly at 7pm and features a score accenting heavily a large variety of show tunes.

Regents offer a great deal of wisdom, experience and fun to anyone one who chooses to try something new. The typical clientele are courteous, educated, well-dressed and pleasant conversationalists. And, boy, can these queens sing. They know their show tunes. If you're a fresh young face, you may be ogled but not often propositioned. And the pedestal you'll be placed upon may just give you another reason to brush up on your Liza.

Your Words: "A cozy party in your own living room." "A piece of Broadway without the $90 ticket prices."

Rising Café

186 5th Avenue @ Sackett Street, Park Slope, Brooklyn, 718.238.8213

As Fifth Ave. in Park Slope becomes more upscale and sleek with each passing month, the Rising Café is keeping a true, grass roots bohemian spirit alive. Lesbian owned and operated, the space could be in the political Mission District in San Francisco. The focus of the café is building community. Frequent benefits are held here, from bluegrass bands playing for Amnesty International to "Dykes on Strike." Live music is featured every Wednesday and Friday, with lots of acoustic guys and gals and local bands serenading the crowd. With spoken word, art openings, and comedy skits, these gals are out to entertain and mobilize queers in Brooklyn.

The atmosphere is homey and pleasant. Butch and femme girls mix with butch and femme boys. Original artwork covers the walls, and there are sofas and board games in the back for anyone hankering for some backgammon or Pictionary. Bulletin boards in the bathrooms let you know everything that's going on in the upcoming weeks. The drink selection is broad — order a German, Belgian or Dutch beer, red or white wine, or a coffee concoction. The jukebox is reliable, playing Janis and Kate Bush, kd and Fleetwood Mac.

Rising Café is probably the best queer place in Brooklyn to go for conversation. It's the kind of place to sip a beer, slouch in your seat, and talk for hours. Truly a unique and welcome addition to the gay and lesbian scene.

Your Words: "A great place to go when I'm feeling restless in my apartment." "I've gotten a lot of writing done there." "My girlfriend and I go all the time."

Rubyfruit Bar and Grill

531 Hudson Street, Between Charles & 10th Streets, Manhattan
Everyday 3pm-2am, Sun brunch: 11:30am-4pm, 212.929.3343

Rita May Brown's Rubyfruit Jungle is one of those books you relish reading in one sitting. It's that great — and so is the Rubyfruit Bar and Grill, which took it's name from the famous queer novel. Just ask Nell Carter, Liz Smith and Lionel Richie of all people, whose pictures hang on the wall of fame near the entrance. The soft lighting and good vibes of this homey bar attract the famous and not-so-famous. Friends and neighbors

inhabit Rubyfruit in droves, whether it's Sunday afternoon for brunch, after work for happy hour or around midnight for a nightcap.

Twinkling red lights, candles and lamps with frilly shades give the upstairs bar a gentle ambiance. There's an unused fireplace behind some

> **"Girls got balls. Their's are just a little higher up."**
>
> **JOAN JETT**

tables, lots of mirrors on the wall, and a cute print of a woman holding cantaloupes over her breasts with the caption "Rubyfruit Melons" over her head. In the back, there's a long cushioned bench under a skylight, the perfect place for getting to know someone. The quality bartenders are too busy to be chatty most of the time, but pleasant and polite. Lesbians make up 90% of the mix, with a few male friends scattered throughout. It's not necessarily a pick up bar, but whose to say you can't buy that cutie at the other end of the bar a drink?

On a street with more restaurants than anything else, Rubyfruit Grill holds its own. Indulge yourself with Sappho's Salad or Michael's NY Strip Steak. After a few drinks upstairs, the hearty portions come in handy. Or if you're too lazy to move from your barstool, they serve Jalapeno Poppers, Baked Brie and a host of other appetizers upstairs. So chow down, drink up, and toast one of the coolest dyke hangouts in town.

Your Words: "After work I like to go to Rubyfruit, sit at a table, rest my feet, order a screwdriver and talk to my friends." "I always take out-of-towners here. The food is delicious."

Saints

992 Amsterdam Avenue @ 109th Street, Manhattan
Nightly until 4am, 212.961.0599

Down the street from the Cathedral Church of Saint John the Divine (hence the bar's name) and the delicious Hungarian Pastry Café stands Saints. An antidote to Chelsea glitziness or East Village faux-bohemia, Saints is a grungy dive bar serving the many staff and faculty members of Columbia University and other Upper West Side locals.

There are no signs outside, no neon lights, no disco balls, no jukebox, and no ambiance. It is a bar stripped down to basic elements — alcohol and places to sit. It's like a Rathskeller on a small college campus — not pretty, but a comfortable place to hang out with friends. The booths with high wood partitions make interaction with strangers difficult, but allow for private conversations. There are soft chairs and couches near the door, where both straight and gay couples converse and cozy up to each other. Straight friends come here to avoid the rowdiness of other het places in the area.

Drink prices are slightly below average. The beer on tap selection is decent, but liquor selection is a bit lacking. Bartenders are friendly, cute but not plastic. Sound system is adequate at best. A house mix plays some nights, and Tuesday is funk night.

If you're looking for no-holds-barred fag mania with booming beats and grinding boys, stay away. If you're in the area with good friends, duck into a booth at Saints and unwind.

Your Words: "A club I belong to meets here sometimes. It's a good place to chill." Graffiti quote from the bathroom: "Just another straight-owned gay bar that loves our $."

Sneaker Bar

392 West Street @ Christopher Street, Manhattan
Everyday noon-4am, 212.242.9830

Sneaker Bar is a gay dive bar straight from the Twilight Zone, unlike any other bar in the neighborhood. Located on West Street parallel to the West Side Highway, it's a strange feeling to be looking out a window in New York and see thousands of cars zooming by. The décor is random, and looks like someone's basement. Sit on the ledge at the back of the bar and check out popcorn popper, the crooked Lite Beer lamp, the inactive pool table, and the large sign that screams "Yes, that outfit does make you look fat," and ponder life.

The crowd mix is unique. Older men often perch here, but hot young guys often come in from the nearby Pier hangout. Tuesday is Ursus Major, a clever name for night of big men who like big men, and there's a two-for-one happy hour throughout the week. Bartenders are accommodating, and the music selection is whatever they want it to be that night — mainly dance mixes, disco or what-have-you. The atmosphere is really low-key and kind of seedy because of the ramshackle surroundings and proximity to lots of porno shops, but it's not really a place for picking up. A back door opens out to West 10th St., where guys stand around and look for a mate.

If you're looking for a beautiful, buff gymbot, this is probably not the place. But if you want to feel like you're on the edge of the earth in New York, especially after a few drinks, the Sneaker Bar can be pretty surreal.

Your Words: "Newcomers often don't get this place, but it's friendly and no pressure." "I hop back and forth from the Dugout to here."

Spectrum

802 54th Street @ 8th Avenue, Bay Ridge, Brooklyn
Th-Sa 9:30pm-4am, 718.238.8213

It's worth the long trip from Manhattan to get to this weekend dance club/bar that screams "Brooklyn!" and screams it proudly. An anomaly amongst car dealerships and Chinese warehouses, Spectrum seems out of place. Once

inside, however, it becomes clear how it stays afloat: good drinks, great people, and arguably America's coolest dance floor — the very same one immortalized in Saturday Night Fever. Even though they don't illuminate the flashing-light dance floor as much as they should, it's thrilling to boogie in the spot where Travolta made disco history.

The place is huge. There's a separate bar area that has a karaoke night on Friday, an enormous lounge area overlooking the dancers, and a small terrace area where you can escape the hullabaloo. Get your mixed drinks at one of the three bars, or a waiter will come around to serve you. Prices are probably higher than they should be in

Brooklyn, but they're still far less than at Manhattan's big clubs. There's a $5 cover on Friday and Saturday, but it's waived on Friday before midnight.

The boys from Brooklyn and Staten Island lack the attitude often encountered at the City's popular spots. The crowd is a delicious mix of Italian Stallions, Boricua boys, lipstick lesbians, and just about every other shade of the pride flag you can imagine, all speaking in the beautiful Brooklyn brogue. The staff is also personable and genuine. The music is not as progressive as you might hear in Chelsea, where DJs are known by their first names. Instead, it's just dance-oriented Top 40, which is ironically refreshing. You may even hear a song from — gasp! — last year! Friday is supposedly retro disco night, but the DJs may break it up a bit.

Essentially, Spectrum is the ideal club for good fun. When you tire of the pretense and pressure of Manhattan, it's nice to know you can be yourself — whoever you are — at Spectrum.

Your Words: "That was fun. We should do this more often." "Where my girls are at! My friends and I go crazy here all the time."

Splash

50 W 17th Street @ 6th Avenue, Manhattan
Everyday 4pm-4am, 212.691.0073

As Chelsea has became more popular over the last decade, so has Splash. Once somewhat rundown and a lot smaller, Splash is now a shiny, sparkling multilevel superbar. With different DJs every night, frequent events and strapping go-go boys, it's managed to maintain its popularity even with the increased competition in the area.

There are two bars and a dance floor upstairs. They're always packed. If you don't feel like shelling out major coins to shake your ass, Splash is a viable option for dancing, although they do charge a moderate cover on the weekends. The DJs are quality, and the music is usually a good selection of the latest club hits. The dance floor is a lot smaller than the Roxy and its counterparts, but there's usually some elbow room. There are hundreds of stools for parking your butt and a few tables for socializing. The downstairs area is more comfortable and civilized. Tiny lamps rest on tables, and boys recline on tall benches. A clothing store, money machine, huge open bathrooms and coat check add to the megabar effect.

No matter what time you show up, there's always something going on. Happy hour swings every day, and the splashbar.com website promises "cute A-list boys" relaxing from their hectic work week. For 10 years Musical Mondays has presented an energetic mix of campy videos and crooning customers — a good alternative to the usual crusty boring Broadway night.

No matter where you are in Splash, you're next to a cute boy. Most are gym hotties, preppy lads, or a combination of the two, along with Jersey boys and some tourists. Like the boys that hang out there, Splash is big, brash, and beautiful.

Your Words: "It's big, there's always lots of boys there, so you really can't go wrong." "This place used to be a dump. What a difference."

Starlight Bar

167 Avenue A @ 11th Street, Manhattan
W-Su 8pm-4am, 212.475.2172

Starlight is not your average East Village bar. Weird, tentacle-like chandeliers hang from the high ceilings. There are no stools along the bar, but there is a wine and champagne menu. An East Village queer bar serving champagne? A few blocks from the raunchy and rowdy Cock, Starlight is more refined and regal.

To the right and left of the door are two little private nooks with velvet curtains and tiny tables. Across from the bar, abstract art hangs above long, slim leather seating. You can choose from seven or eight beers on tap at the bar including Kirin and Hopjack. Along with the champagne, the mostly female bartenders will help you choose between an apple martini, an extensive selection of liquor, and $6 glasses of good wine. The back room is more subdued with cozy corduroy couches, a stage and a DJ setup in the corner. Every night hosts a different but talented DJ, and all seem to have a knack for playing the right music at the right time. On Wednesdays and Thursdays the small stage is used for cabaret singers that play to a mixed crowd. On Fridays and Saturdays well-dressed 30-something boys pack the place so they can longingly eye each other. Sunday is ladies night where lots of hot lesbians end their week.

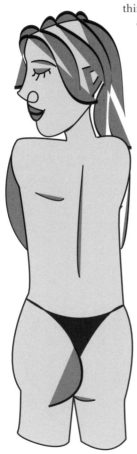

Having recently come under new management (they also run nearby Wonder Bar), with a rumor that they might open up an outdoor seating area in the back, Starlight is a very cool bar that may get even better.

Your Words: "A great place to take a date after dinner." "A fresh alternative to the other divey bars in the Village."

Stella's

266 W 47th Street, Between 7th & 8th Avenues, Manhattan
Everyday noon-4am, 212.575.1680

If you're sitting at the bar at Stella's, and a strapping young buck starts caressing your chest and asks how you're doing tonight, it's not because you're all that. He's probably a hustler. Well, how about that! Stella's is a welcoming island of raunchiness and mayhem in a sea of corny movies-turned-Broadway shows. While the boys-for-hire are a main attraction here, the grand old place has a lot more to offer.

The upstairs room is spacious and quaint. Broadway posters line the walls, and the pool table in the back always attracts a crowd. Happy hour is a lengthy noon to 8pm every day, and bartenders serve the drinks with a wink and a smile. 23-year-old very fine examples of rough trade circle the bar, many of them glued to their cell phones as if they were managing their stock portfolio. Men old enough to be their fathers sit and drink, checking out the scenery.

The downstairs room is a different story. There are lots of go-go boys giving the audience boners like their lives depended on it. These are not detached, model wannabes that stand atop the bar and barely work up a sweat. They are aggressive amateurs who will wave their assets inches from your face. Sometimes their routines are choreographed, sometimes they work the entire room, sweat flying everywhere while the salivating crowd cheers them on. The mostly black and Latino dancers are always enjoying themselves. Even if you're not the type to stuff dollars down G-strings, you'll be taking out you're wallet before the night is over. If you've just paid 60 bucks for theatre tickets and the show sucked, spend a lot less at Stella's and get your money's worth.

Your Words: "In the suddenly sweaky-clean NY scene, Stella's keeps me sane." "There's nothing else like Stella's in the city."

Stonewall Inn

53 Christopher Street @ 7th Avenue, Manhattan
Everyday 2pm-4am, 212.463.0950, www.eStonewall.com

Sure, it's not the original neighborhood pub that made history, but it is a living testimony to the courage and pride that erupted here on July 27th, 1969. The current owner Dominic and his partners are due all the proper respects for their loving restorations. Are history lessons necessary? It's been called everything from the birthplace of the liberation movement to Queer Mecca.

The front room walls are covered in blown-up newspaper clippings of the fateful event, and pictures from that era. Gracing the cozy old brick and wood interior are the familiar images of drag queens and butch leatherboys, reflecting the clientele du soir. It's got that "all belong here," homey kind of vibe that is so relaxing after a day's work. Take a place in line to shoot a round on the red felt pool table while taking advantage of the two-for-one happy hour special, or cozy up next to someone in one of the booths. One plus is that no matter where you are in the place, you can actually hold a conversation without having to shout, since the music is not only tasteful but also kept to a comfortable volume.

> "Most men who are not married by the age of thirty-five are either homosexual or really smart."
>
> **BECKY RODENBECK**

Saunter to the back and you'll find that the rear room is slightly cooler in spirit, with a second bar, a blueish tone to the light, and surely a sexy bartender holding court. You will imagine that this is the room to score a furtive grope or overt smooch with that sexy new someone.

Perhaps best of all, the management has finally scored its hard-sought cabaret license. By the time of this pressing, the dance floor upstairs will be in full tilt, with yet a third bar and plenty of fresh tunes to satisfy the diverse crowd that it'll doubtlessly attract.

It's your favorite underpants, your easy chair, and your momma's meatloaf all rolled into one totally easygoing, comfortable experience.

Your Words: "The recent renovations really enhanced this place. It's now the nicest bar in the West Village." "The best place to bring out-of-towners. Cultural and fun!"

Tool Box

1742 2nd Avenue @ 91st Street, Manhattan
Everyday 8pm-4am, 212.348.1288

If you are feeling claustrophobic and looking to escape the confines of your tiny, outrageously priced New York apartment, the Tool Box is not for you. Sandwiched into a room smaller than most efficiencies, lots of horny Eastsiders who don't want to bother with a sojourn to the main gay breeding grounds in the city flock to this seedy little bar. The front door, unmarked by name or street number, resembles an opening to a meat closet and befitting the initial impression, Tool Box proves a deli display of what the Upper East Side has to offer.

Besides Brandy's, the nearby piano bar, Tool Box is the only real pick up joint in the area. The cruisy Ruppert Park also gives the randy local folk more of a reason to stay at home. The dank and musty bar area is lit by dim phallic shaped emergency lights lining the side wall as well as the raunchy flicker of hardcore porn pouring down from the television. A few wobbly candlelit tables are scattered along the back and the bathroom is kind of grungy, but if you want cleanliness go to Chelsea. The Tool Box is for the East Side what the Cock is for the East Village. The backroom is always pulsing with prospects. In the basement, the small dark room often contains hidden treasures.

Prices are semi-steep and the place isn't much to look at, but people don't come here for the ambiance. Plenty of pretty young things straddle the stools of the bar in anticipation of straddling someone below. Maybe tonight's your night.

Your Words: "You never know who you'll pick up here." "Get drunk. Get laid. And get to bed before midnight."

Townhouse

236 E 58th Street @ 2nd Avenue, Manhattan
Everyday 4pm-4am, 212.754.4649

Bar owners Rick Unterberg and David Pellegrene cater to a large portion of the NYC gay crowd. One or the other owns stock in Regents, Heaven, and Townhouse to name a few. While the techno and house beat of Heaven tends to attract the younger, successful 20-somethings of the West Village and Chelsea, Townhouse and Regents attract the older, more established NYC gay elite from the upper regions of Manhattan.

> "I wouldn't recommend sex, drugs or insanity for everyone, but they've always worked for me."
>
> **HUNTER S. THOMPSON**

Nestled between ritzy and industrial neighborhoods, the Townhouse atmosphere is a mix of country club sensibilities and Ab-Fab madness. The establishment contains three cherry wood bars, brass rails, crystal lighting fixtures and posh, comfy couches. Framed photos of polo players and golfers line the walls. From the back of the multi-sectional first floor, the soft sounds of the piano waft through the various nooks and sitting rooms that give Townhouse its (Donald Trumpish) homey feel. Considered primarily to be a cabaret bar, Sinatra and show tune-themed nights add a campy, fun flavor. Drink prices range from five to seven bucks, and the Sunday to Wednesday happy hour from 4pm to 7pm offers three-dollar well drinks.

While mum is always the word and overt soliciting is never tolerated, the moneyed crowd tends to attract the younger, more enterprising hustlers. Although not a "backroom," the downstairs bar offers a bit more privacy and seclusion for getting down to business. Townhouse is a small society unto itself. While there may not be any yearly dues, social standing and occupation tend to play important roles in determining "membership" status. Townhouse is filled with attractive, fit and successful men that feel they've earned the right to pick their friends and lovers.

Your Words: "An upscale place where the older gentleman don't try to look younger." "A subculture of New York nightlife, without the shadiness and commotion."

Two Potato

143 Christopher Street @ Greenwich Street, Manhattan
Everyday 4pm-4am, 212.255.0286

At the end of the Christopher Street strip, Two Potato is a delicious mixture of fierce drag queens, go-girl go-go boys, and Afro-American and Latino men whooping it up and having a good time. To get a taste, glance at the bulletin board outside the bar advertising upcoming events. Recently, Queen Bitch Luscious, Sugga Pie Koko, "The Real Energizer Bunny" Lady Jasmin, and Avantis Ova-King all the way from Norfolk, Virginia were scheduled to appear. If you're a drag fan but tired of seeing the same old routines around town, Two Potato is worth a visit.

The go-go boys on Wednesday on Sunday start out on stage, and then roam the crowd for tips. It's refreshing to see go-go boys that aren't standing and posing away from the masses. The music is a great mixture of new and old R&B, hip-hop and some gospel mixed in. They don't have their cabaret license, but people can't help but dance in their seats. A tall, handsome bouncer will take your $5 cover when he's not playing the video game near the door. The bar is near the pier, and boys are always hanging out nearby, blasting Hot 97 from their cars and generally carrying on. It's like the Queer as Folk scenes when everybody's partying in droves on the streets of Pittsburgh, except they're not all white.

> "Well, well, well! Stubb knows him best of all, and Stubb always says he's queer; says nothing but that one sufficient little word queer; he's queer, says Stubb; he's queer—queer, queer; and keeps dinning it into Mr. Starbuck all the time—queer, Sir—queer, queer, very queer."
>
> **CARPENTER**
> *About Capt. Ahab in Moby Dick*

If you're bored with your regular bar and are looking for something different, spend a night at Two Potato and nearby Chi Chiz. You'll spend the night talking, laughing and making friends.

Your Words: "These drag queens have me rolling in the aisle." "The only place for go-go boys."

Ty's

114 Christopher Street, Between Bedford & Bleeker Streets, Manhattan, M-F 2pm-4am, Sa-Su 1pm-4am, 212.741.9641

A self-described Gay Cheers, Ty's redefines the word "cozy." A third of the space is taken up with the bar itself, which works in its favor as there's plenty of room for the world's friendliest bartenders to keep up with the remaining two-thirds of the place, typically filled to a comfortable capacity by 9:30 pm nightly.

Established in 1972, Ty's is a community staple, home to the late 20s to early 50s crowd of laid-back professionals and their ilk. Any variety of dialect or accent might be found in here; Ty's fame has spread across both oceans. The tone is always jovial and upbeat. Friends shout across the packed house while lovers quietly sip their drinks in one of the two spacious window seats up front — perfect perches to catch the action in or outside the house.

Ty's isn't a sports bar as such, but they do support two teams of guys who like to bat balls: both the Tygers and the Buddies softball teams call Ty's home and, win or lose, all are well-received at this nest after the last pitch has been thrown. Camaraderie is king here, whether you play or not.

The prices are reasonable and the portions ample for the price, especially if you're in the mood for the bartender's choice of the day. Ask for the choice and expect a response quickly fired back ("Bourbon!") from the well-toned John, who pours happy hour suds on Tuesday and Thursday afternoons.

Happy hour as defined by Ty's lasts until midnight on Monday and Tuesday, by the way, so it's a great pick for starting up the week right as well as closing it out in good form with great guys.

Your Words: "I've come with longtime friends here almost every week and have a ball." "I feel like part of the gang here."

View Bar

232 8th Avenue, Between 20th & 21st Streets, Manhattan
M-F 3pm-4am, Sa-Su 1pm-4am, 212.929.2243

No, the View Bar isn't atop a skyscraper over-looking the regal island of Manhattan. In the back alley through a window there's a painted backdrop of Miss Liberty, the Twin

Towers, the Chrysler building and the other likely suspects, reminiscent of your 11th grade school play. It's a funny gimmick, but one the View doesn't necessarily need. It stands alone as maybe the friendliest bar in Chelsea.

View seems spacious for a small bar. At the entrance there's a huge window overlooking bustling Eighth Ave, and nearby tables and seats for people watching. The long bar stretches down to a back room with a pool table, more tables and the aforementioned "view." The pool table is on top of a spacious platform with breathing room, so you don't feel like you're going to poke someone's eye out with a cue. Along the walls are televisions showing series of soft-porn stills that look out of place. The bartenders are amiable and cute, and serve up strong concoctions. The $1 Forbidden Fruit shots on Sunday are tasty, and happy hour starts at an early 3pm during the week. Nightly DJs tucked into a cave-like booth are enthusiastic and creative. If you're bored and lonely on a Monday night, catch an encore of Queer as Folk at 8pm.

> "A couple in a sexual experience is happy for that moment. Then very soon trouble begins."
>
> **DALAI LAMA**

The crowd is mixed — men and women, young and not so young — and the atmosphere is open and welcoming. Unlike other gay bars, the interior is visible from a main drag, and probably attracts lots of passerbys who've never heard of it.

The View may be trying to be the newest highfalootin' Chelsea hotspot, but in spite of itself it's just a quality, normal neighborhood hang out.

Your Words: "My favorite happy hour in Chelsea. The one bar in the area I can kick back in." "A good place to have a drink after dinner in one of the many restaurants in the area."

The Web

40 E 58th Street, Between Park & Madison Avenues, Manhattan
Nightly until 4am, 212.308.1546

The Web bills itself as "New York's only Asian dance club, cabaret, and lounge." In a city with such a high percentage of East Asians, it's baffling that there aren't more. The place has been around "since forever," in the words of one doorman. A long, steep staircase leads down into a balcony bar area, which looks down onto the dance floor. Every seat provides a view of the dancers below. The Web is renowned for its dancers — young, hot, boyish Asian guys with great figures and great moves. They're worth the price of admission. The enthusiastic crowd keeps the dance floor active. Aesthetically, The Web wins big design points: the lighting is tasteful and sensual, and the sound system is top notch.

"Men's World" on Saturdays is a showcase for different talent, including drag queens and house DJ Emperor Moseley. Sunday night features a Karaoke night almost as fun as Pieces in the West Village. Happy hour attracts a large, somewhat conservative after work contingent. There's a $5 cover charge Thursdays and Fridays; Saturdays it's $10. Drink prices are typical, but DJs periodically announce specials.

The atmosphere is pretty relaxed. Since the crowd is predominantly Asian, the club attracts groups of friends looking for a place to hang out, as well as single boys looking to hook up. Whatever your purpose for the night, The Web is always a blast.

Your Words: "Those dancers are the subject of many a fantasy." "This is my favorite place to chill out after work. It's a different world."

Wonder Bar

505 E 6th Street @ Avenue A, Manhattan
Everyday 6pm-4am, 212.777.9105

While most East Village bars are grungy and a bit rough around the edges, Wonder Bar adds some elegance to the mix. Once a mishmash of kitschy memorabilia, the interior is now simple and sleek. Rich red drapes are hung up high, permitting just the right amount of ambient light to leak out, with strong simple tones of red and yellow painted on the walls. Opposite the bar there is a row of padded bench seating against the wall with small candle-topped tables interspersed throughout. And there are actually private, relatively clean bathrooms! The space is cozy and comfortable.

> "The Bible contains six admonishments to homosexuals and 362 admonishments to heterosexuals. That doesn't mean that God doesn't love heterosexuals. It's just that they need more supervision."
>
> **LYNN LAVNER**

The after-work crowd is small as happy hour is only 6pm to 8pm, but if you're looking for a quiet place to talk, Wonder Bar is sublime before the crowd rushes in. By 11pm or midnight, the place is bulging at the seams with attractive 25 to 35 year olds. With a different DJ spinning everything from space disco to hip-hop, the mood is friendly and surprisingly multicultural. In general, the music here is more mature and diverse than the usual gay disco fare. Both guys and girls are mingling here, with girls coming earlier and guys staying later. While lots of cruising takes place in such close quarters, most seem to be searching for LTR material rather than a one-night stand. Drink prices are slightly higher than in the surrounding gay watering holes.

If there's no room on a Friday or Saturday at Wonder Bar, which happens often, there are lots of viable options within a ten-block radius (Boiler Room, Phoenix, Starlight, which is owned by the same management). Even after many years and bold changes, Wonder Bar is garnering its share of attention for serving up a lively and hip slice of New York nightlife.

Your Words: "The DJ's really set the tone." "It's not just the white-bread crowd. People come from all over the city."

The Works

428 Columbus Avenue @ 81st Street, Manhattan
Nightly until 4am, 212.300.3501

The Works has this really appropriate neon sign announcing it's presence — the old Monopoly 'Water Works' logo. The blue and red neon dripping faucet against the bar's black-out windows is the only discerning feature that sets the bar apart from the surrounding company: Starbucks, countless boutiques, and typical Upper West Side storefronts.

Now a cynic might read too much into the flaccid nature of the unmistakably phallic sign, but the 20-year old Works is a reliable, sexy neighborhood joint. Regulars are friendly and often know each other well, but aren't complacent — they're not afraid to approach a fresh face. The bartenders help facilitate hook-ups by assigning each person a number tag. If you see someone you like, you write a little note addressed to that person's number on bar-supplied paper, and slip it into a glass. Cute and practical.

The Works attracts lots of faithful regulars, middle-aged but not exclusively. Mostly Upper West Side white and somewhat well-to-do, but not exclusively either. On any given night, you can come across old-time scene queens, young Latino studs, and hot (and flirty) bartenders. They're all chatting away, watching 80's vids on any of the myriad televisions, and most importantly, having fun.

The solid black and blue Euro lighting scheme and lofty ceilings give a feeling of high altitude. The sound system is great and usually blaring pop fare, but the speakers are positioned high enough to allow for easy conversation. The front bar area is less narrow than most places, and there's a large back room for congregating. There's also a little downstairs area with space enough for a spontaneous encounter. The bathroom's spacious and clean. Drink prices are average.

Just a block from the Museum of Natural History and a block from the subway, The Works enjoys a great location. There aren't that many bars in the area, especially with this loyal of a following, so a visit here is a no-risk venture, whether you want to pick up or just hang out.

Your Words: "I've been coming here for 20 years, and there's still some surprises." "It's a good location, a real neighborhood place, but still open enough that there are lots of new faces."

"It has been proven that the pig is the only homosexual animal. As this perversion is most prevalent in pork-eating nations, it is obvious that it gets into your genes through the meat."

TASLEEM AHMED
Islamic Missionary, from a Muslim mission in Galaway, Ireland; First quoted in London's "Freethinker" magazine

Dance Clubs

▼

Since legendary disc jockey Alan Freed spun Top 40 hits at the Brooklyn Paramount, New York City has been home to some of the most influential dance clubs the world has ever seen. Celebrities did "The Twist" at the Peppermint Lounge in the 60s, David Mancuso and the Loft helped invent the discotheque in the 70s, DJ Kool Herc tore up the Bronx in the 80s, and Junior Vasquez brought the house down at Sound Factory in the 90s. So where are the best places to work up a sweat these days? The next section provides info on what, when and who's gonna be at the club nearest you.

New York's dance scene is always vibrant, volatile and eclectic. Experience world-famous DJs flown in for the weekend, and up-and-comers learning their craft on a weeknight. Clubs always plan "gay nights," but if the DJ is good, there are bound to be some gay boys and girls checking it out. Make sure to pick up a copy of HX or Next at the nearest bar — clubs advertise special nights in the free magazines, and often offer a discount on the cover charge if you bring the ad. Of course, if you go early — 10pm to 1am depending on where you go — you can take advantage of drink specials and low cover, but at the risk of being the only one dancing until the crowd comes.

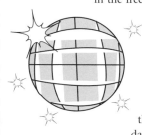

There are often long lines, sometimes artificially created to make the club look packed to the outside world, but be patient. Usually once you get inside, it's worth it. Above all, stay positive, listen to the music, and dance your ass off.

219 Flamingo

219 2nd Avenue @ 13th Street, Manhattan
Tu-Su 10pm-4am, Sa 10pm-7am, 212.533.2860

Since so many NYC queers gladly pay the exorbitant covers at the many trendy Chelsea clubs, the East Side has been left by the wayside. In 219 Flamingo, New Yorkers now have a feasible alternative to the near identical throng of West Side clubs that have dominated the area for so long.

With the exception of Tuesday and Wednesday, the hardcore hip-hop nights, 219 Flamingo is primarily a cruisy, gay dance club. The Top 40 Thursday dance party Pop Rocks! is the most popular of the gay nights and is hosted by DJ Gerson. The two floors of the small bar are usually packed from wall to wall with twentysomethings who have no problems admitting that 98 Degrees are cool. Flamingo Fridays are home to one of the most popular and enduring lesbian parties in the city...the Clit Club. The likes of Madonna, Salt-n-Pepa and Queen Latifah have listened to DJs Darryl and DM spin old school R&B, hard house and a bit of underground techno. Saturdays are more mixed as the majority of the straight contingent mingle in the large downstairs bar and lounge area amidst the gritty sounds of modern and classic rock. Upstairs the house grooves of Steve Travolta satisfy the hoard of homos who have gathered en masse to dance their asses off on the small dance floor.

Flamingo provides its clientele with everything that makes a dance club a good dance club: great music, fair drink prices, an attentive, helpful and friendly staff and a casual atmosphere. Take any popular Chelsea club and subtract the drama and pretension from the equation. What's remaining is probably soon to be one of NYC's most popular dance clubs. Dance all night. Drink all night. Cruise all night. You won't want to leave.

Your Words: "Flamingo has a real New York feel to it; it's special and unique without the manufactured facade created in most of the other clubs." "Grinding against some hot guy while N'Sync sings 'Bye Bye Bye' is too much fun."

BarCode

46th @ Broadway (next to Virgin Megastore), Manhattan
Everyday 11am-4am, 917.893.9967

While the adult arcade Barcode has only been open for a year, its Australian owners opened five similar successful clubs in their homeland before trying their luck in the Big Apple. So far their gamble has paid off. This place is just fun. Purple, pink and blue neon lights cover the bar, walls and pool table, and add to the jovial and raucous setting. Movies play constantly on the 50-odd TV screens that line the walls of the entire arcade. DJ Scott (who also hosts Saturday nights at Studio 54) and DJ Roberto are just two of the many fine disc jockeys who spin an array of hip-hop, house, techno and 80s mixes in 30-minute sets, so that a well-rounded rotation of tunes is played throughout the night. Myraid new and classic video games and a young, attractive clientele are part of what sets Barcode apart from the over-priced tourist traps of Times Square. The outgoing staff serves strong, reasonably priced drinks. Typical bar munchies — burgers, nachos, etc. — range in price from $5 to $13. Dollar draft happy hour at Barcode can be a cheap unconventional way to end the workday.

> **"Don't they know I'm a gay man trapped in a woman's body?"**
>
> **MADONNA**

What better way to forget your ugly boss than by playing Ms. Pac Man while drinking rum and cokes? Wednesdays and Fridays tend to be the mixed nights, and a handful of queers can be found here at almost any time.

Barcode is conducive to a casual date or getting drunk with pals. This funhouse is also known to attract an ever-growing list of NYC stars. MTV Studios is located across Broadway, and the likes of Backstreet Boy Kevin Richardson, Carson Daly, Tom Green and even Blink 182 cross the street to play a video game or two here. Barcode plans to get their cabaret license and the upstairs game room will be transformed into a nightclub. There aren't many clubs in the nearby vicinity, so the place should explode. A crowd of young, tipsy 20-year-olds in Times Square could trigger a plethora of problems associated with a liquor establishment, but the ID policy here is strict and security is airtight. Touristy it can be, but lots of locals also enjoy the mayhem at Barcode. Think of the pick up lines you could use at an arcade.

Your Words: "The modern adult version of Coney Island." "Dinner and a movie gets boring. Barcode is stylish enough to impress a date, but entertaining and down-to-earth at the same time."

Blu

161 W 23rd Street @ 7th Avenue, Manhattan
M-Th, Sa-Su 4pm-4am, F 4pm-8am, 212.633.6113

Whoa, Nelly. If either cruising or dancing is your scene, you've come to the right place. The customers at Blu make no qualms about what they've come to do. The minute you walk into the door, myriad curious eyes turn to face your way. Standing against the bar, dozens of tops glance seductively across the way at the veritable buffet of bottoms lining the walls and black leather couches. So all that's left to do is assume the position, or if you are desiring the simple pleasures of good music, push through the thick haze of smoke and hormones and seldom used pool table to the small but chic, strobe-lit dance floor in the back.

Besides the ultra popular "Faggot Feud" hosted by Mona Foot and Dick Dawson (a twist on the old popular game show where a handful of homos are pitted against each other for $250 in cash and prizes), Blu is all about the dancing. With a smattering of go-go boys on Fridays and Saturdays, Blu showcases some of New York City's finest deejays. Anthony VLantis spins fierce techno and house music every Tuesday night. On Fridays and Saturdays after the go-go performances, Erik Reyes and Randy Bettis bring the party to its pinnacle as they master the turntables with a psychedelic twist.

Unlike such quintessential Chelsea bars as Splash and the new Heaven, Blu is a less crowded, less sweaty, and after a few drinks, a less selective crowd. Although they may be the leftovers from the dining table of the Chelsea elite, the beauty and muscle of this crowd is nothing to scoff at. The drama, however, may be. And it's there in full force...but what would a Chelsea bar be without it?

With a little less ado than most Chelsea bars, the environment is more conducive to either an always ethereal night of dance or a tasty night of tricks and treats. It's all up to you. Just be sure that the set of Blu balls that you go home with is not your own.

Your Words: "I come for the music. The beautiful boys are just a bonus." "Hot boys...hot music...and, if you play your cards right, a hot night of sweaty sex."

Centro-Fly

161 W 23rd Street, Between 6th & 7th Avenues, Manhattan
Everyday 10pm-5am, 212.539.3916, www.centro-fly.com

Tom Sisk, co-owner of Centro-Fly, is no stranger to the more glamorous world of NYC. He not only used to be involved in the film industry, but also has a large stake in Aubette, an upscale city lounge/restaurant located in Gramercy. In Centro-Fly, he serves up a bit of the fabulous for those who rarely have the opportunity to taste it.

Centro-Fly is not your average club with smelly bathrooms and trashy atmosphere. While it may cost $20-$30 just to get into the doors of the club and up to $12 for a well martini, Centro Fly has more than enough to back up the somewhat hefty prices. The Friday GBH party, running for 3+ years, is considered by NY Magazine to be "one of the best nights out in the city." Fat Boy Slim and the Chemical Brothers have performed at Centro-Fly, and movie and music producers have used this venue on more than one occasion to shoot scenes for both the big and small screen.

> "I'm coming out! I want the world to know, gotta let it show."
>
> **DIANA ROSS**

While the architecture of the establishment is predominantly 60s European Op-art, modernity is most certainly not something that CF lacks. Over the span of two spacious floors, the expensive and effective sound system controls the club. A who's who of international DJs spin a mix of house with a soulful, underground edge every Thursday, Friday and Saturday. The eclectic, worldly cuisine served in the Tapioca Room gives CF an additional healthy twist. Every night until 4am, tired dancers and chronic loungers can sate their palates and get a second wind. The themed rooms located throughout the multi-level club offer patrons temporary R&R after or between sets of hardcore dancing.

The average age of this racially and gender mixed

crowd is mid-twenties, but the steep prices and exclusivity of the large contingent of VIP clientele tend to stave off
the less moneyed crowd. There's also a strictly enforced
50/50 gender ratio that eliminates the common problems
that arise in large single-sex groups. CF is alive with com-
fort and attitude. If you're looking for a little bit of both,
be sure to stop by the ATM first.

Your Words: "CF allows you the opportunity to dance,
relax or dine. How many other places in NYC offer that?"
"I feel special here."

Escuelita

301 W 39th Street @ 8th Avenue, Manhattan
Th-Sat 10pm-5am, Su 7pm-5am, 212.631.0588

This place is hotter than a spicy enchilada
from Taco Bell, and has a much larger selection of meat from which to choose. Located
just outside tacky Times Square, Escuelita
serves up a nightly celebration of men of color
and their queen-size admirers. Over the past
five years, Escuelita has become one of the
most reliable clubs in the city. The publishers
of both the Latin Inches and Black Inches have

created a club as sexy as their magazines. The sensual
groove of Ray Lorenzo's hip-hop, salsa and house party
(Thursday-Sunday) and Steve "Chip-Chop" Gonzalez's
Latin House, hip-hop and reggae fest (Thursday and
Friday) move the crowd until the wee hours of the morning. The all-night performances of the big and beautiful
go-go boys, including Black Inches cover man Jason, create an atmosphere thick with carnal desire. Once a
month, the club hosts a party for both magazines in a
meet and grope session that features magazine signings
and performances.

On any evening a great mix of black, Latino, and
white boys bump and grind on an enormous dance floor
surrounded by two large bars, couches, lounge tables and
three small performance daises. At some point during the

evening, the music stops, everyone sits Indian-style on the floor, and the drag queens take the stage. They'll have you rolling in the aisles. It's sometimes difficult to separate the trannies from the women that make up a respectable portion of the kaleidoscopic crowd.

Escuelita has been known to encounter a semi-violent skirmish here and there. In their May edition of "Escuelita" magazine, they published their own complaint on this sporadic problem. But mostly the atmosphere is homey and congenial. This place has flava, character, pizzazz and a large bouquet of burgeoning, long-stemmed pricks. If you want a taste of quintessential gay New York nightlife, all you need to do is say those three little words: Yo quiero Escuelita.

Your Words: "There's more cock in this place than in all of Kentucky." "It's rare to see so many guys and girls of all backgrounds coexist peacefully in one place."

Fun

130 Madison Street @ Mechanics Alley (under the Manhattan Bridge), Manhattan, Nightly until 3am, 212.929.6060, www.MotherNYC.com

When you hear the words "sexy robot," do you think of Arnold Schwarzenegger in Terminator 2? If so, the Click and Drag show may not be your cup of tea. Sexy robot, as well as cyberslut, rubber, gothic, post-apocalyptic, leather, vinyl and glam nerd are just some of the ensembles and identities that the freaks at Fun inhabit. No khakis, jeans, sports wear or generally boring clothing is allowed.

The reason for the strict dress code is twofold. While you may be welcomed with open arms once you make your way inside, the party itself is exclusive. Click + Drag serves the "other" section of the Lifestyle listings. The crowd isn't fully straight or gay identified and doesn't want to be. The clothing regimen also serves as a safety mechanism for a night with a potential for disruption. Only those who understand and celebrate the artful vision of non-conformity can enter, so that every third Thursday of the month NYC's most fabulous can frolic freely in the funky fetish flavor of Fun, without anyone judging them.

The hosts and producers of Click + Drag are Rob Roth, designer and producer of Blondie's No Exit album and tour, and Kitty Boots, fashion designer for such stars as Lil' Kim and Gwen Stefani. In a dark, remote area of Chinatown, they've found a venue that supplies the

ambiance for the crowd they're attracting. Four in-house projectors illuminate the 18 video monitors with underworld sexcapades. Two roving stealth cameras as well as spy-cams in the opposite sex bathrooms allow full view of everything these boys, girls and boy-girls have to offer.

Every night has its own theme, be it tranny, domination or punk night. DJs Load Rezenhand (of the Throb music empire) and Sammy JO spin alternative dance and rock. Live performances often stir the droves into rhythmic frenzies. And kink is everywhere — on the televisions, parading on stage, and mingling amidst the hot throng of beings thriving in an orgy of fetishism.

The five-dollar cover is a small price to pay for such a rich and sexy celebration of diversity. It gives anyone the opportunity to bring to life their secret desires. The guts and imagination it takes to forego the Gappers and Banana Republicans for something more dangerous and real is plenty reason to slap on some jeweled undies and heavy eye make-up and celebrate a night of freedom.

Your Words: "Who'd ever think you could find beauty in such outright and blatant deviation?" "We were never being boring."

Heaven

579 6th Avenue, Between 16th & 17th Streets, Manhattan
Everyday 4pm-4am, 212.243.6100

If faith is something missing from your life, look no further than this new NYC gay house of worship. Amidst wall to wall white and mirrored interior, angelic faces and heavenly bodies decorate three floors of pure bliss. Here you'll find St. Peter and his friends waiting in full force and ready to get biblical.

There are three steps to spiritual enlightenment at Heaven. Find your way to the first floor meet-and-greet setting. The well-lit room, bright white marble bar and stained glass mirrored walls as well as the lounge/stage furnished with couches and end tables enable easy access and vision of a potential companion. Once company is found, progress to the second floor, where the room darkens, mirrors and sparking blue diamonds cover the walls, and the music and dance floor allow a bit more intimate inspiration. Only the true (and VIP) believers can complete the journey to the third floor, the climax of this holy experience, where privacy replaces prudence and virtue is fed to the dogs.

> "As long as the music's loud enough, we won't hear the world falling apart."
>
> **DEREK JARMAN**

Hector Alfonseca, Dean Merritt, and DJ Vito are just a few of the many renowned DJs that Heaven has on its payroll. Thursday's Latin Dancefest, the industrial house and techno of Friday's DJ Alex Lauterstein, and the retro-80s celebration of Heaven's third floor Saturdays all draw an eager crowd of Chelsea boys, Midtowners and Eastsiders. The crowd consists of youth and its admirers, especially Saturday night, sponsored by GayCollegeParty.com. Afterwards, party at the dorm!

Heaven is a must for any gay local or tourist. Admittance is free four nights a week and for a small pittance and penance ($5-10) access is granted on the weekends. Heaven combines a dash of Splash, a little bit of Chase and a whole lot of Roxy. The music is hot and the boys are slammin'. And, whether or not you go home with someone, you most likely will leave this place feeling very blessed.

Your Words: "I'm addicted. People have been waiting for Heaven to open for awhile, and we're not disappointed." "Impure thoughts run rampant through our minds and sins are committed nightly. Heaven always lives up to its name!"

DANCE CLUBS

Hush

17 W 19th Street @ 5th Avenue, Manhattan
Everyday 5pm-4am, 212.989.4874

After working the doors at Studio 54 as security and assistant manager, Steven Steckel has taken his knowledge of legendary NYC nightlife and poured it into his new dance club/restaurant Hush. Steckel offers a powerful combination of eclectic American cuisine and some of NYC's finest entertainment. Hints of the old Studio 54 pervade the club. The stage and spacious dance floor are surrounded by a large bar, dining tables and cozy little nooks and booths furnished with velvet couches. The cabaret-like main room is offset with a cozy, yet psychedelic lounge housing a second bar, crimson couches and walls lit with bleeding lava light transparencies.

Offering a little flavor for everyone, themed nights include: the popular Monday Salsa After-Work Party hosted by resident DJ Henry Knowles and featuring both free salsa lessons from 6:45pm to 8:00pm, and Friday's Latin Fusion, headed by promoters Carlos Antonio and Chi Chi and featuring hip-hop, reggae, and R&B spun by the likes of Fish and Ed Swift. Daily happy hour features half price drinks every Tuesday to Friday from 5pm to 8pm as well as a complimentary buffet.

Hush makes no secret that its gay clientele is a very valuable asset to this primarily straight restaurant/ bar/dance club. Although the once popular Friday "gay night" is no longer part of Hush's repertoire, the establishment does host a Saturday and Sunday tea dance once a month. Known for her gigs all around the country, including the Black Party and White Party in NYC, DJ Susan Morabito rocks the tea dances with techno and house mixes. These special Sunday gatherings are often filled with shirtless muscle boys in search of a viable prelude to the hopping Sunday night dance scene. While only one day a month is labeled "strictly" gay, the typical weekly crowd is often an equal mix of breeders and bottoms.

But, no matter the crowd, Hush has something to please them all.

Your Words: "The perfect date — dinner and dancing all in one spot." "Upscale...Trendy...Mixed. Great Music. Great Dancing. Great Vibes"

Limelight
660 6th Avenue @ 20th Street, Manhattan, Everyday 10pm-early morning, 212.807.7780, www.limelight-tunnel.com

In a society whose motto is "Out with the old and in with the new," clubs come and go like fashion. The wrecking ball of progression has erased so much of what was celebrated in years passed. Limelight, on the other hand, is one of the few places left standing that fights this notion of "moving on to something better."   Progressive in its own right, Limelight serves as a substantial bridge between the past and the future.

In an old, abandoned church on 6th Avenue, Limelight has enjoyed the longest run of any club in the city. Parties such as Cocoon, Trust the DJ, and Gate Crashers draw 1000's of people each weekend. DJ Heaven, one of England and Australia's top house DJs, spins every third Friday of the month and has amassed a large US following. Although popular because of the renowned DJs, the Gothic and Tudor architecture (high cathedral ceilings, intricate stained-glass windows and maze of staircases and hallways) bring thrillseekers from miles around out to enjoy the club's rich sense of history and culture. For a $20-30 cover, anyone can experience the larger-than-life feeling of Limelight. Dance in the main room, Chapel Room or HR Giger room, lounge in one of the many side nooks and rooms scattered throughout, or observe everything from the extended upper balcony which hovers above the cavernous dance floor. Vertigo!

Every Sunday at Limelight, Promoters John Blair and Mark Berkley present DRAMA, a 21+ gay dance party featuring a mix of trance, house and techno spun by James Anderson and a host of other guest DJs. Fridays and Saturdays tend to attract the younger crowd, the rave clothes and the glow sticks, as the minimum age drops down to 18. Even though Sunday's group tends to average in the low to mid 20s, the crowd is filled with old souls. The beautiful, ethereal, eerie Limelight has seen it all. Disco queens, club kids and maybe even your Mom and Pop have felt the bass shiver in their bones here. Who knows when it will close again, so come here and experience it while you can.

Your Words: "A sexual and spiritual romp." "Standing on the balconies and watching the teeming masses dance is always cool."

Meow Mix

269 Houston Street @ Suffolk Avenue, Manhattan
Everyday 5pm-4am, 212.254.0688, www.meowmixchix.com

Meow Mix is the place in NY for dykes to dance. Even with all the publicity and notoriety the club has generated over the years, it's stayed true to its roots. It's still the coolest East Village dive, with frequent drink specials and low covers.

Meow is one of the only consistent venues for queer music in New York. Legends Sleater-Kinney, Team Dresch, and Exene Cervenka have rocked the house here, and lesser-known local artists continue to broaden their audience at Meow. The theme nights have always been pretty great. Will Xena Night continue now that she's been heartlessly taken off the air? Hopefully the festivities on the second Tuesday of every month will keep the warrior princess alive and kicking for a while. DJ BK-Brewster spins a more eclectic mix than most of the gay boy clubs on other nights. The downstairs room had a reputation for flesh and mayhem back in the day, but since then Meow has been forced to convert it into a comfy rec-room-type place. Still, with delicious go-go dancers and the hottest women grinding away on the dance floor, Meow is still the sexiest place Houston Street has ever seen.

Like the best of the East Village, Meow Mix is a cool mix of laid back flavor with some edginess and unpredictability thrown in for good measure. After all the publicity, Meow could have fell victim to its own success. Happily, it's still the same old happening club.

Your Words: "It's the kind of place that puts a smile on your face while you're dancing." "...where I find my girlfriends."

Nowbar

22 7th Avenue, Between 12th & 13th Streets, Manhattan
Tu-Su 11pm-early morning, 212.726.8168

Nowbar is a dark, seedy place that draws the NY underground from their caves. The music is loud, and the crowd plays hard. Every Wednesday and Sunday DJ Unknown or DJ MK master hip-hop, reggae, house and R&B mixes on the turntables. While Wednesday tends to be a mix of both gay boys and fly girls, Sunday is typically a hetero event. Thursdays and Saturdays are hosted by married promoters Gil T. Pleasure and Gloria Wholesome and feature a healthy dose of trannies and their chasers, as well as some amateur performances. On select nights, if you take a deep breath and suddenly feel dizzy, be wary of Mary Jane. And, no, she isn't the resident drag queen in the joint. Nowbar is the proud venue for a few non-traditional recreational activity events, sponsored by the Doobie Brothers. Cover charges for these nights range anywhere from $5-10.

If romance is what you are looking for, be sure to visit the upstairs lounge. The dimly lit, secluded bar area with booths, pillows and a semi-private room is sometimes home to lap-dancing trannies as well as any other amorous patrons. While the downstairs is booming with rhythm, lots of patrons can be found sitting along the couches, booths and stools that line the rock and ivied walls of the large bar room and the smaller and cozier corner nooks. Make no mistakes — Nowbar is a dive, a little hole in the wall, something the drink prices ranging from $5-10 may not indicate. If you don't feel like paying the semi-steep alcohol prices, relax, take a seat, and bum a smoke.

Your Words: "I hate clubs that are too hyper and eager to please. Nowbar is chill." "If you like overbearing light shows and the same dance music week after week, don't come here."

Pyramid

101 Avenue A @ 6th Street, Manhattan
Th-Su 10pm-3am, 212.462.0977

Eighties theme night 1984 has been thrilling Madonna wannabes and Andrew Ridgeley fans since — well, practically since the 80's. It's currently location is Pyramid, and with 80's mania at an all time high, the night gets more popular by the year. After 11pm, Pyramid is wall to wall with young, enthusiastic gay boys — some of whom were still in their crib when Frankie was telling us to *relax*. No need to dress up since you'll be sweating to the oldies. If you're an 80s freak, there's no holding back.

The retrofest is commanded by a rotating cast of

amateur DJs, including the up-and-coming Chips Duckett. Music ranges anywhere from vintage Janet to the Go-Gos to Pet Shop Boys. Pyramid provides ample space for a dance fiesta with a large dance floor, as well as a stage for the more flamboyant fags, but, while classified as a dance club, Pyramid ultimately has more of a dive bar feel. The downstairs lounge area is more conducive to conversation, and you might hear Cure and Depeche Mode there if you need to get away from the hectic pace. Open mic night on Sundays tends to draw a sizable group of East Villagers and starbound queens. Performances range from lip-synched versions of "I Will Survive" to amateur renditions of "Oops, I Did It Again." Sunday also features a hip-hop showcase of both popular and underground urban beats.

> "I feel like a million tonight – but one at a time."
>
> **BETTE MIDLER**

If you're looking for a "night at the Roxbury," this isn't it. But if you want to lose weight by flailing uncontrollably to the happiest music ever written in a low-pressure setting, 1984 at Pyramid could become an addiction. The drinks are cheap, the cover is reasonable, and the formula is simple. Put on a smile and spin right round like a record, baby.

Your Words: "If you're not into the hardcore dance scene but like to dance, 1984 is perfect." "My mouth hurts from smiling when I leave here."

Roxy

515 W 18th Street @ 10th Avenue, Manhattan, 212.645.5156

We've all heard of Roxy. Roxy *is* New York City nightlife, gay or straight. The grandiose and seemingly far-fetched tales which often follow a night at this legendary hot spot often seem more like fantasies or aggrandized myths of another world. The stories are true. Experience the gathering of the

city's most beautiful men, the larger-than-life sexual energy that engulfs the room, music spun by some of the world's most famous DJs hypnotizing all who listen, and, did I mention the gathering of the city's most beautiful men?

John Blair's Roxy Saturday night is one of the oldest and most enduring gay parties in the country. It's the White Party and Mardi Gras combined, celebrated once a week instead of once a year. Two of the world's most renowned DJ's, Victor Calderone and Peter Ralphoher, spin the house and techno that give this club its kick. On Wednesday, put on your pink leotard and fall on your ass at the only roller disco in NYC.

Situated in the middle of one large room, the city's largest dance floor is packed with 1000+ men at a time. Go-go boys seduce the crowd with their sexy and seductive sways, but in a room full of scantily clad, perfectly built men, you may have trouble discerning who is who. And even though there are four bars to service you, be bold and act beautiful. Otherwise, you'll wait for a drink.

A large lounge area lays adjacent to the dance floor and is covered in a large tent-like enclosure where you can recover, relax, or fondle new friends. A second, but much smaller room up the steps beside the main bar offers a birds-eye view of the festivities below, as well as a second, smaller dance floor.

Roxy is dripping with sweat, lust, and euphoria, and all the ephemeral pleasures that gay men celebrate most. It's a must see for any tourist or local alike. The $20 cover charge is just a small tithe to pay to the gay gods who inspired the gayest and most decadent dance party in the city.

Your Words: "How do you describe something this fantastic?" "The feeling you get as soon as you walk in this place is more powerful than words."

Spa

76 E 13th Street @ Broadway, Manhattan
Tu-Sa 10pm-4am, 212.388.1060

Every Thursday night, a diverse flock of NYC's finest gathers for the Ultra party at Spa. Drag queens, leather men, butch dykes, breeders, Chelsea boys and the kitchen sink come together for a night that epitomizes the best of what the city has to offer.

As chic in design as it is in ambiance, Spa sports a neon-lit waterfall that cascades behind the small front bar. House beats pound in your bones on the nearby dance floor, with the likes of Alex Lauterstein and DJ Merritt setting you free. In the White Room, with its white booths, walls and bar, Girlina and Lady Bunny diversify the musical repertoire with a large selection of hip-hop, house and classics. Although not designed as a dance floor, the aisle separating the two rows of booths is often packed with dancing queens and shirtless boy toys.

While the $20 cover as well as the $7-15 beers and drinks may be a bit pricey for a Thursday night, the selection of men is worth the extra coins. Keep in mind that the average age of the crowd is around 25 and percentage of body fat is a much lower number. Spa has a very exclusive feel and attitude. The VIP room in the center of all the action, furnished with Italian leather couches and champagne buckets, is an indication of the exclusivity.

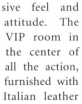

Spa has the verve of Splash, the attitude of Roxy and all the makings for a brand new night to celebrate NYC life and music.

Your Words: "...a rainbow of flavor." "This place is filled to the brim with fashionistas and their admirers, sipping cosmos and dancing all night."

Speeed

Over the past few years, the Friday night party at Speeed has been known as Club La Mancha and Papicock. Recently, the party was renamed Players Club. While the pseudonyms have fluctuated, hosts Darren and Mike have consistently drawn a large contingent of the city's hottest masculine Latino men (and boys to gawk at them) to celebrate one of NYC's sexiest dance parties. Resident DJs T-Pro and Louis Correa spin a mix of hip-hop, R&B, house and classic house on the two dance floors situated on the first two levels of this three-story establishment. On the roof, clubgoers can dance, mingle, lounge, breathe some fresh air, and of course, cruise. The club is full of seductive, erotic energy.

Player's Club turns things up a notch with go-go boys this side of paradise. For an extra $5 at the door, a wristband entitles patrons to an all-night, hot-cock-in-your-face sextravaganza. The dimly lit side room, known as the Lap Dance lounge, features 8-14 impossibly hung dancers who gladly offer up their goods for a few moments and a few bills. The sessions are both hot and monitored; the staff at Speeed never allows things to get too out of hand. If the boys aren't enough to get your blood pumping, the night also features such gimmicks as a big dick contest, dance strip-offs, and lap-dance strip-offs, as well as racy, yet tasteful Pornformances. And if you're an early bird, a $5 cover allows you to enjoy an open bar from 11pm-midnight. "The Player's Club" will hopefully last for a long time. With enough sausage to fill the meat closet at your local A&P, who'd ever want it to end.

Your Words: "Cute, masculine Latin men. I want them all. Now." "My body tingles just thinking about it."

Tunnel

27th Street, Between 11th & 12th Avenues, Manhattan
Everyday 11pm-8am, 212.695.4682

Promoters and clientele of Tunnel will tell you that what matters most at their favorite NYC dance club is the music...and they're not lying. In an enormous abandoned warehouse in the meat packing district with one large dance floor, two smaller ones, and various other nooks and side rooms, everybody dances until they hurt on Saturday night.

Two parties, Almost Famous (straight) and Kurfew (gay) mix, mingle and intertwine throughout the night. And the party gets started as soon as the first few walk in the door. It jams early and doesn't fizzle out until the music stops. The Kurfew "side" boasts the most trippy of dance floors. The room is decked out in neon-lit pillars, myriad mirrors, as well as furry walls and ceilings. Amidst the glow sticks, plastic pants and bare midriffs, a barrage of hard house and techno accentuates an already psychedelic feel. The main floor often jams with live bands and performances.

Situated just beyond the reach of the hard-core clubbers on the dance floor below, an upstairs room plays host to a large urban crowd dancing to the sounds of hip-hop, progressive and old school. DJs Jackie Christie, Michael T. and Kitsch and Camp give the musical repertoire its diversity and edge. Preppies, borough boys and Chelsea boys salt and pepper both crowds. With all this, the $20 cover charge seems a small price to pay.

The bar that spans a large area of the main floor is rarely packed with patrons because everyone is dancing. Also, large amounts of underagers (18-20) frequent this party. While the very young clientele would serve as a wet dream to many, others find them annoying. The drama and pettiness is known to be in full force here. But if you come for the ambiance and music, the night will prove carefree and worthwhile.

Your Words: "Space enough to do your thing, no matter where you are." "It's stood the test of time." "Maybe the last classic dance space in New York."

Vinyl

6 Hubert Street @ Hudson Street, Manhattan
F-Sa midnight-10am, Su 4pm-midnight, 212.343.1379

Not all NYC clubgoers need alcohol to have a good time; the music is what matters most to them. Vinyl gladly celebrates this faction of the club scene with a dry venue. Water and soda pop sate the palates of the crowd, while the soulful vocals, gospel, trance and house quench their spiritual thirst for rhythmic euphoria. Who better to keep the night alive with deep, progressive house and trance than DJ Danny Tenaglia, one of earth's most in-demand DJs? He spins every Friday for the Be Yourself party. For the Club Shelter party every Saturday, Timmy Regisford is the man responsible for the mosaic of garage classics and house. During the diurnal Sunday Body and Soul extravaganza, Danny Krivit, Francois K and Joe Clausell share their time mixing a large variety of vocals, gospel and house. The DJs create the feel and respond to their audience. It's like back in the day.

Sunday may be designated the gayest of nights at Vinyl. It's one of the only places in New York where the music is the main focus, so people from all walks of life come here to lose themselves. Space is limited! Other than a medium sized dance floor, only the small VIP lounge and Red Room allow an escape from the masses that pack the place nightly. Vinyl is dimly lit, mysterious and thriving with sexual vibes. The wide variety of dancers, the look of the place and the obsessive attention to the music make Vinyl unpredictable.

Your Words: "If you're visiting and only have time for one night out, this should be your choice." "You don't need drugs here. Vinyl is a drug."

Warehouse

141 E 140th Street, Between Grand Concourse & Walton Avenues, Mott Haven, Bronx, 718.992.5974, www.clubwarehouse.com, Call or access website for updated schedule

There's been a lot of press lately about homo thugz. The Village Voice and Vibe magazine have reported on boys of color that maybe don't identify as gay or queer or whatever, but still sleep with other guys. Where do homo thugz go, along with queer boys and girls who prefer hip-hop over the latest dance remix? The Warehouse is the spot right now. A huge club in the South Bronx, it attracts droves of hip-hop heads and house music freaks from all over the tri-state area.

The Warehouse has multiple dance floors, a stage for fierce go-go boys, a huge lounge area with decently comfortable seating and a restaurant/store that sells everything from chicken wings to laser key chains. Lord knows there are some beautiful bodies grinding on the dance floor, but the emphasis is on dancing and the music, not on how you look. DJ Unknown, Andre Collins, Frankie Paradise and many others spin current jams and obscure old school, as well as classic and current house. The crowd is made up of mostly boys, but since there aren't many clubs like the Warehouse in New York (or anywhere for that matter), the ladies get down here, too.

The South Bronx isn't the safest area in the world, so feel free to take a cab if you're unfamiliar with the area. Once you survive the long line and get inside, the vibe is safe, inclusive and fun. Don't shy away! In a town where clubbing seems a bit stale lately, The Warehouse is a revolutionary place to be.

Your Words: "It's the Paradise Garage all over again." "I travel 125 miles to get here every week. It's worth it." "Nothing else in the city even comes close."

Cabarets & Piano Bars

▼

Been to one-too-many dive bars in recent weeks? Are your legs tired from dancing? Are you and your friends sitting around playing the "I don't know. What do you want to do?" game? Come to a cabaret show or a piano bar and sing along with some of the most talented performers in the country. From the sweet melodies of Rodgers and Hammerstein to the comedic stylings of *The Producers*, New York is home to a rich Broadway history. But maybe you don't have 80 bucks to plunk down on a ticket to *Les Miserables* or *Annie Get Your Gun*. What better way to relax than to order a vodka and tonic, saddle up to the bar and listen to an ingenue sing "Some Enchanted Evening" or "Don't Rain on My Parade"? In addition to Broadway tunes, cabaret singers often cover popular jazz standards and music. There's something for everyone. Most places attract a healthy mix of queers and straights. The performers always take care to make sure everyone's participating and having a good time. So call up your sophisticated lady, and come on along and listen to the lullaby of Broadway!

Arci's Place

450 Park Avenue South, Between 30th & 31st Streets, Manhattan
Lunch: M-F 11:45am-3pm, Dinner: M-Sa 5:30pm-11pm, Call
for cabaret times, 212.532.4370

Offering delicious Italian food, a romantic setting, and cream-of-the-crop cabaret singers,
Arci's Place is a perfect destination for a classy
night on the town. Owner John Miller offers a
talented selection of award-winning perform-

ers seven days a week. Whether it's Margaret Whiting
telling us she'll love you "Come Rain or Come Shine," Jim
Caruso making us smile with "If I Only Had a Brain," or
the beautiful Saundra Santiago having fun with "Laziest
Gal, Daddy," each night is magical and entertaining.

The cabaret room in the back is cozy but not too
small, seating about 100. Arci's Place takes his name from
16th century artist Giuseppe Arcimboldo, and the décor
is inspired by his striking images. The performers croon
to the sounds of a Steinway, and the lighting and sound
quality are always exceptional. The sophisticated, loyal
audience comes from in and outside the city. Five days a
week Arci's features established artists, and the other two
days provide opportunities for gifted up-and-coming
performers.

The dining room in front is casual yet elegant.
Appetizers run from $8 to $12, and entrees are a reasonable $10 to $18. Vegetarians can feast on a scrumptious
selection of pastas and salads, and meat lovers can enjoy
Veal Parmigiano or free range chicken dishes. The staff is
attentive and professional. Arci's holds two-for-one
happy hour from 5pm to 7:30pm, and surprisingly a convenient takeout menu available from 7am to 10pm.

Arci's Place is all you would expect from an East Side
premiere cabaret and eatery. It's a reliable choice for
impressing a date or to experience top level, experienced
NYC performances by candlelight.

Your Words: "When I want to escape the mania of the
city, I come to Arci's." "...the new kid on the block."
"...always exceptional."

Brandy's Piano Bar

235 E 84th Street @ 2nd Avenue, Manhattan
Everyday 4pm-4am, 212.774.4949

Brandy's hasn't changed much in the thirty years it's been around, and that's a good thing. The old-fashioned stencil on the windows advertising "Same Old Brandy's Good Time Saloon" makes the entrance look like part of a movie set. Inside, a wooden bar crammed with stools takes up half the space, and a piano room with tables and benches takes up the other half. Next to the piano, a placard reads "Out of courtesy to the pianist, please refrain from smoking at this table." The poster above the piano reads "Incredible friendships begin at Brandy's." The general atmosphere is as benevolent and gracious as the signs.

The attractive, effusive bar staff double as the performers, and belt out a wide variety of rock, Broadway, and jazz tunes every day after 9:30pm. Billy Joel tickled the ivories here way back when, and many current stars of stage and screen have sung for the small, devoted audience. On weekends, the bar side tends to be gay, and the performance room leans hetero. Everyone gets along swimmingly. The song selection is upbeat, and the staff is engaging. Smiles are on the house! Brandy's gets packed weekdays after 10pm and after 9pm on weekends. The crowd generally consists of 35+ year old men, with some young male and female theatergoers in the mix.

> "I am an actor. Of course I can play a heterosexual!"
>
> **SIR JOHN GIELGUD**

If you lived on the Upper East Side, Brandy's should be your regular hangout. Chatting with friends and acquaintances during the 4pm to 8:30pm happy hour is a great way to unwind. The owner is Irish, and the place has that congenial Irish feel to it. Pull up a stool, knock down a pint, and croon along with the song.

Your Words: "A good low-pressure place to drink." "I've been coming for 20 years. Home away from home."

Danny's Grand Sea Palace

346-348 W 46th Street, Between 9th & 10th Avenues, Manhattan
Lunch: W, Sa & Su 11:30am-3pm, Dinner: Su-Th 4pm-midnight,
F-Sa 4pm-1am, 212.265.8130

The stretch of 46th St. from 9th to 10th Ave. is sublime. Colorful awnings from endless restaurants adorn the tree-lined street. Each evening Broadway fans stroll arm in arm looking for food and further entertainment. Smack in the middle of the block across from Don't Tell Mama's is Danny's Grand Sea Palace, a quality restaurant, Broadway piano bar, and cabaret in one location. The staff works hard to provide a memorable evening of melody and fine dining.

In Danny's Skylight Room, the piano bar section of the establishment, Mac Award-winning Jerry Scott engages the crowds with Broadway standards and lots of personality on Thursday, Friday and Saturday nights. On Sunday, sometimes bartender Scott Ailing blows the audience away with a powerful voice, along with partner Charles Lindberg, who plays on other nights. Their performance of selections from "Secret Garden" will rip your heart out. The bar is mostly gay, with some straights wandering in during peak tourist hours. Members of the theatre community hang out here, as much as any other piano bar in the city. The cast of regulars here is amiable, entertaining and loyal.

The cabaret room hosts established artists as well as up-and-coming gems. The atmosphere is classy and relaxed. The restaurant is seafood heaven, offering frequent lobster and crab specials. Whether your Aunt Bea is in town to see Phantom and you need to entertain her further, or you're in need of a drink, song and some company — Danny's won't let you down.

Your Words: "Never an attitude here. And the performers are always quality." "You can't go wrong with Jerry Scott."

Don't Tell Mama

343 W 46th Street, Between 8th & 9th Avenues, Manhattan
Everyday 4pm-4am, 212.757.0788

An inexhaustible, fun-no-matter-what kind of place, Don't Tell Mama is one of the city's long-standing cabarets. Located only a stone's throw away from the theatre district, there is always a strong supply of after-the-show patrons usually in the Broadway mood before walking in to Mama. The talented wait-staff takes advantage of the musical giddiness, along with a number of singing regulars.

Don't Tell Mama features a piano bar up front, where sing-alongs begin every night at 9:30pm. A main stage in the back features a wide variety of cabaret acts including original musicals, stand-up comedy, talent showcases and more traditional revues. Many performances are experimental, and involve the willing audience. Cover charges vary per show, and there's the usual two-drink minimum per person. Reservations are accepted, and credit cards are not accepted. There's a daily happy hour with half price drinks from 4pm to 7pm if you need to get drunk before the show.

The décor is swank and the atmosphere welcoming. A bunch of predominantly gay locals keep the night rolling along with boisterous participation. The mixed crowd ranges widely in age, from straight Midwestern couples to local theatre aficionados. The attractive, good-natured, experienced bar staff are powerful singers and make an effort to include everyone in the festivities. For example, they'll have the whole bar harmonizing to tunes from Rent or Rodgers and Hammerstein until three in the morning. Winner of numerous MAC Awards (Manhattan Association of Cabarets and Clubs) year after year, Don't Tell Mama is a reliable destination for musical fun.

Your Words: "Perfect place to bring your straight friends." "This placed is packed with talent. It's entertainment that's both fun and sophisticated."

Duplex

61 Christopher Street @ 7th Avenue, Manhattan
Everyday 4pm-4am, 212.255.5438

While Chelsea reigns supreme as the gay neighborhood in New York, the old haunts in the West Village still pack a punch. Take the 1/9 to the Christopher Street stop, walk up the stairs, and within view is the deliciously schizophrenic Monster, the newly refurbished Stonewall, cowpokes poking at Boots and Saddle, and the Duplex. Unlike the other Sheridan Square landmarks, this charming piano bar attracts a very diverse crowd. On a Friday night, the place is packed with lesbian couples, straight out-of-town townies, raucous gay boys, and your grandmother. And when I say packed, I mean packed, at least on weekends. The staff is as good-natured as they are talented, and fans keep coming back.

> "It is better to be hated for what one is than loved for what one is not."
>
> **ANDRE GIDE**

On most nights, the bartenders take turns pouring drinks and crooning alongside the piano. The song choices are as unpredictable as the clientele. One minute you'll hear the Bee Gees, the next it's Rodgers & Hammerstein, and then out of nowhere someone's channeling Axl Rose.

Diva Free Tuesdays are extra fun, and on weekends Gerry Diffenbach has been engaging the crowd for years. Wednesday's Open Mic is often a blast. Although they do have a sidewalk café for stretching out, the piano bar is small and audiences have no choice but to be drawn in and sing along. There's also a bar, jukebox and pool table in a quieter upstairs room. Look out the small windows for a good view of Sheridan Square.

If they don't mind crowds, take your distant cousins here when they come to visit. Weeknights are less crowded but just as merry. The Duplex is gleefully unpretentious and is appealing for all ages.

Your Words: "The bartenders introduce themselves by name. I always feel welcome." "Check out the headshots on the wall. Where else can you find Shaneen Doherty, Emilio Estevez and Yoko Ono in one spot?"

Judy's Chelsea Cabaret

169 8th Avenue, Between 18th & 19th Streets, Manhattan
Everyday 4pm-4am, 212.929.5410, www.judyschelsea.com

It's only natural that there's a cabaret in Chelsea. For three years, Judy's Chelsea has charmed its way into the hearts of the neighborhood gay folk. The front area is the piano bar, with ten long tables seating the crowd from work or a boys night out very comfortably. The bartenders/performers are cute (sometimes cutesy), kind, and talented. The atmosphere is loose and spontaneous. There are two entertainers daily, and most perform relatively recent material to cater to the youthful Chelsea crowd. A snack menu is available after 10pm for music fans with the munchies.

The cabaret room can be seen from the piano bar through a glass wall. It seats 50 comfortably and serves as a restaurant area when there are no performances scheduled. The back wall is also a large window, and overlooks a garden. The stage area is large, giving performers some breathing room. There's something happening in the room seven days a week. There's a cover plus a $10 food/drink minimum, and reservations are strongly suggested. It's the only cabaret in the neighborhood, and the place gets packed, especially on the weekend. Somewhere between fancy and laid back, Judy's Chelsea is a unique alternative to a night of Chelsea bar hopping.

Your Words: "Glad I don't have to travel too far anymore to check out quality cabaret." "Judy would have been proud."

Lips

2 Bank Street @ Greenwich Avenue, Manhattan
Everyday 5:30pm-midnight, Sun brunch: noon-4:30pm,
212.675.7710

Hidden in the residential districts of the West Village is the jewel encrusted treasure box called Lips, where the food and drink take a back seat to the fabulous dames who serve them up. An evening at Lips is dragtacular dining at its most decadent!

The flashy trashy themes vary from evening to evening. There's far too much creative energy in the house to get repetitive. Highlights include Tuesday's Drag Karaoke with the gossamer songstress Chashetta, who recommends that the nervous try a frozen

cosmopolitan or six to get over their stage fright. Wednesday hosts the notorious 'Bitchy Bingo' night, with winners receiving theater tickets to various local productions, tee-shirts, etc., but it's the catty banter between hostesses Linda Simpson and Yvonne Lame that is the real prize here.

Five nights a week, your mixologist is the magnificent Frankie Cocktail, whose presence rivals that of her doppleganger, Dolly Parton. Any given evening she'll emerge from behind her bar to grace the patrons with a titillating rendition of "9 to 5," and the crowd response is always as big as her bosom.

Atypical of other similarly themed restaurants, the food here is nothing to powder your nose at. Prices run the gamut from average to high, but the quality is always well above par, and the portions ample. Recommendations include the Candis Cayne (chicken BLT, $7.50), the Coco La Chine (grilled yellow fin tuna, $19.00), or the Fantasia (black linguini with caramelized mushrooms, $12.50).

Summer and Christmas seasons are particularly busy, and at any time of the year reservations are recommended, particularly with parties over four. Even on the weekend, when the management opens up the lower floor, it's a safe bet that the house will be packed with knowing locals and tourists looking for something that's totally unavailable in Montana.

It's a perfect place to take your out of town visitors — if you like them, it's a great treat, and if not, there's plenty going on to keep you from having to talk to them! If you're a fan of flamboyant drag or just out for sensational dining with a twist, Lips is a scintillating experience for all the senses.

Your Words: "It's hard to keep drag fresh in this town, but Lips manages to make me laugh every time." "I told my grandmother I play Bingo every month. Little does she know. Linda and Yvonne are a hoot."

CABARETS & PIANO BARS

Rose's Turn

55 Grove Street, Between 7th Avenue South & Bleecker Street, Manhattan, Everyday 4pm-4am, 212.366.5438

A loud, raucous, smoky piano bar, Rose's Turn features a terrific singing staff, alternating pianists, and an open mike policy every night of the week. If screaming along with complete strangers and sitting shoulder to shoulder with residents and tourists alike sounds like the NYC experience you're looking for, then keep Rose's in mind for your next West Village outing.

The downstairs space is intimate to say the least. Seventy people squeeze into a small room that would comfortably fit 40. West Village rent is expensive! Most of the patrons are gay, male and fun, so the crowding is easily excused. On weekends Rose's becomes the village's only rock-n-roll piano bar. Bill Graves plays jazz standards and hits from the last three decades, and Broadway veteran Terri White keeps the place hopping with tunes like Mustang Sally and Proud Mary. You may find yourself ordering more drinks than you should just for the added bonus of having the waitresses sing at your table with amazing intensity and verve. The weekends of course are especially busy, and during the summer months the full-house quality spills over into just about every night of the week.

Upstairs from the joyous chaos is a tiny cabaret room where performances take place nightly. Everything from comedy showcases to improv to musical revues can be enjoyed at a fairly low cover. Recent performances include *Elephant Man: The Musical*, *Around the World in a Bad Mood*, and *The Improvoholics* — nothing boring here. Expect to be part of the show in such close quarters.

One of the oldest piano bars in the city, Rose's Turn is a sister club to midtown's Don't Tell Mama. Both clubs are as entertaining and unpredictable as Mama Rose herself.

Your Words: "The staff is welcoming and gracious. And very witty!" "A fun and classy place to hang."

Sex

▼

You can still have lots and lots and lots of sex in New York. Yes, recent hypocrite mayor Rudolph Giuliani has clamped down on the city's scintillating sex dens and glistening gloryholes while cheating on his wife in Gracie Mansion. But in a city of phallic skyscrapers, constant energy, and some of the hottest men on the planet, you will find a way to get off. From the hunky men in towels at 82nd Street Club in Queens to Wall Street closet cases relieving stress at Ann St. Entertainment Center, there is lots of fun to be had. The next section provides descriptions of safe places for men to shoot a load. If you want to further explore some of the covert, ever-changing spots to have sex, crusingforsex.com is an amazingly complete reference for information on hundreds of cruisy parks, bathrooms, subway stops, etc. Remember to be patient, don't be shy, and clean up after you're done!

82nd Street Club

40-33 82nd Street, Between Roosevelt & Baxter Avenues, Jackson Heights, Queens, Su-Th 2pm-2am, F-Sa 24 hours, 718.396.3945

Welcome to the 82nd Street Club, the only always accessible sex club in the outer boroughs. To get in, pay for a temporary pass that gets you in five times within about a month, or the more expensive yearly membership. Pay more if you want a locker to put your clothes in, or your own private room. The attendant is kind enough to give you a towel, condoms and lube, and your key with a wristband since you probably won't have any pockets while strolling around the corridors.

There are over 100 clean rooms inside, equipped with a small cot attached to the wall, and a light. Boys with rooms usually stand in their doorway checking out the trade passing by, or lay on the bed with the door open while boys without rooms peek their heads in, waiting for an invite. Guys here generally range in age and style, though a healthy percentage of the temporary residents at 82nd Street are young black and Latino men, many of them muscular and masculine. Most guys walk around sans clothing, but some keep their shirts on. The drunk, horny after-bar set around 4am on the weekend is eager to please, and there's usually a decent amount of guys earlier in the night. There's one room with bleachers and pornos showing, and sometimes action takes place. Of course, there are showers for cleaning up afterward.

> "I wish I had taste buds up my ass."
>
> **ROBERT PATRICK**
> *playwright*

Chances are if you're patient at 82nd Street, you'll find what you're looking for. It's pretty hardcore, and not for the faint of heart. There's little socializing, no pictures on the walls, no alcohol, just dick. It's about 10 blocks from the Roosevelt Ave. subway stop, and near a few good bars — Music Box, Friend's Tavern and Atlantis 2010. A visit to the 82nd Street Club is a satisfying way to finish up a night in Queens.

Your Words: "It's like you're in a porno. I can't stop coming." "I like coming here, shutting out the rest of the world, and getting off."

Ann St. Entertainment Center
21 Ann Street, Between Nassau Street & Broadway, Manhattan
M-F 7am-11pm, Sa 10am-11pm, Su 10am-7pm, 212.267.9760

Ann St. Entertainment Center is quite entertaining, and maybe the center of the best casual, standing-up sex in Manhattan. A paltry $9 gains you entry to the upstairs lair. To your right is the Jimmy Swaggart Room (ha, ha, ha) where men sit around and watch pornos with their clothes on. It feels like a Super Bowl party where the game is a runaway and everybody's bored. Straight ahead is a larger, brighter room with guys straddling chairs and watching more pornos. That room feels like an AA meeting.

Go through that larger room, and there are booths with either pornos or wrestling videos playing. What's with the wrestling in these places??? Anyway, there is always action here, day or night. Pent up businessmen come at lunchtime and after their hectic workday. Latino, Middle Eastern, Black, Asian and other international beauties come from around the area or on their way back to their wives in Brooklyn. No matter what your taste is, you'll find it here. Generally

SEX

there's no hassle from the staff, and no attitude from the customers.

Upstairs there's a good mix of porn, S/M paddles, dildos and probably the best selection of sexually themed board games in the city. Go figure. All in all, a great opportunity for explosion at the tip of Manhattan.

Your Words: "I had the best three-way here." "The best place in the city to get off."

Christopher Street Books

500 Hudson Street @ Christopher Street, Manhattan
M-F noon-4am, Sa-Su noon-6am

A longstanding landmark in the West Village, Christopher Street Books still delivers sex and mayhem on a street that used to be all sex and mayhem ten years ago. Other than Harmony Video down the street, Christopher is the only place to see some dick on the gayest street in America.

Upstairs Christopher Street features a solid selection of pornos, along with the weird law-enforced percentage of "mainstream" videos. You can get your condoms and lube here in a pinch also. At the counter, you'll notice a $10 admission sign. Admission to what?

Once through the magic door, you'll see a couple of bathrooms, a bench with a couple guys chilling, and around the corner to the right, a lone booth with a porno viewing screen. To the left, descend the long gray stairwell to find 20 or so individual booths with porno screens inside. The videos range from hardcore action to clothed men wrestling. If there are more than 20 boys there, the extras will be jostling for position trying to man their own booth. The lucky extras will be invited inside a booth by a like-minded horndog. It isn't pretty, but it's a lot prettier than other quick fix options in our post-Giuliani sex-starved city. This place attracts all

> "Sex is the only thing worth living for."
>
> **ROBERT MAPPLETHORPE**

kinds — from older guys looking for a thrill to younger boys on the make after too many cocktails. Of course it gets packed during late night hours, but since there's not much else like it around anymore, there's usually a healthy crowd no matter what time of day. A staple of the West Village scene for 32 years, Christopher Street Books will hopefully thrive for many years to come.

Your Words: "My savior." "The last bastion." "The staff is actually very knowledgeable and helpful."

East Side Club

227 E 56th Street @ 2nd Avenue, Manhattan
Everyday 24 hours, 212.753.2222

If you find yourself feeling a bit randy at Regents, or if you've gotten hammered at the Tool Box and need to screw, get a room at the East Side Club and scratch that itch. Next to a Chinese restaurant on a quiet street, East Side is in a neighborhood where the residents have maids and personal investors. Thus the clientele here is considerably older than in other sodomy palaces, although lots of 20-30something guys are in on the action also. Hundreds of rooms are located on three floors. You can get lost! Upon entry, a cute boy escorts you to your locker, at which point you disrobe, and run amok. If you want to save a little money and rent a locker rather than a room, chances are you'll be invited into someone's temporary lair.

The main floor features a small sauna, lockers and showers. Taking showers in the open is reminiscent of high school. Yum! Guys trample their wet feet through the halls, so watch your step. Stroll through the corridors, peer into the rooms, and check out bottoms with their butts pointed upwards, and daddies stroking their dicks. The mood here is relaxed and low pressure. Men will chat in the sauna and in the porno room. All shapes and sizes are represented here, so no need to feel shy about your body type as you walk around in a towel. Getting lonely

SEX

in your hotel room? Is porno getting old? Head over to the East Side Club, forget your troubles and get your groove on.

Your Words: "It's hard to leave." "My personal sexual playland."

Gaiety

201 W 46th Street @ Broadway, Manhattan
Shows @ 1:30pm, 3:30pm, 6pm & 8:30pm daily, F-Sa 12
dancers at 6:15pm, 9:15pm & 12:15am, 212.221.8868

The Gaiety's main claim to fame is being featured in Madonna's infamous Sex book. You're unlikely to find the pop superstar here these days, but if the thought of muscular, well-endowed boys waving their cocks in your face sounds appealing, Gaiety is probably worth the $15 admission. Once a dirty, horny jackoff theater, it's been forced by the city to clean up its act. Patrons sit gazing at guys that make Chippendales look homely, but can't touch themselves or anyone else. Until they get home.

The crowd ranges in age and ethnicity. Couples often come together for a thrill, and curious females show up once in a while. Before each striptease, pretzel rods, chips and virgin punch are served in the lounge. The strippers hang out nearby around a South Park pinball machine before they go on, and customers hover and salivate. Each act first performs an actual "tease," keeping some clothes on before they exit the stage. Three minutes later they come back and take

it all off. The guys in the front row seats are close enough to sniff, so get there early for a good seat. It's worth it.

In between shows, they play porno flicks. For some reason the audio sounds like its coming from a transistor radio in the back, but no matter. Again, there's no relieving yourself, but it's not unforeseen that you'll meet someone here. The men at the Gaiety will be the subjects of your masturbatory fantasies for months to come.

Your Words: "I never thought I'd be that close to God." "My favorite show on Broadway."

Harmony Video

139 Christopher Street, Between Hudson Avenue & Greenwich Street, Manhattan, Everyday 24 hours, 212.463.0657

Down the street from Greenwich Village's reliable sex den Christopher Street Books, Harmony Video is a worthy spot for sex toys, pornos and buddy booth action. Upstairs Harmony features every sized dildo you could imagine, penis pumps, leg cuffs, "video head cleaner," a pretty good magazine selection, and a lube called Analese. The staff will help if asked.

The video selection downstairs is extensive and organized. It's really easy to find whatever you're looking for. Titles are divided by numerous studios and also by genre — fetish, black and Latino, etc. Many video stores don't respect their product and shove the pornos on the shelves, but Harmony knows their stuff and caters to the customer. Prices can be steep, but that's the studios' fault. Older titles can be a lot cheaper. Newer tapes that are cheaper are often of poorer quality.

There's a row of six buddy booths toward the back, patrolled by a staff member. Like most booths in the city, they accept credit cards and bills. There's a two-inch crack between each booth for viewing your neighbor. The crowd ranges from black men and Latinos that hang out around the west part of the street, to older Village locals, an after-work crowd, and drunk boys from one of the many nearby bars.

There are 11 bars within a five-block radius not to mention a huge gay residential community, so Harmony isn't normally hurting for customers. Unlike a lot of the buddy booth stores around town, Harmony actually offers a worthy selection of sex-related merchandise.

Your Words: "It's not hard to sift through the twinks & jocks to find movies with beefy hairy guys." "I shop here for lube and videos, and there are fringe benefits."

J's Hangout

675 Hudson Street @ 14th Street, Manhattan
Everyday midnight-8am, 212.242.9292

The J in J's Hangout stands for jacking off. This dingy sex den in a flatiron building near the meat packing district used to be a lot seedier. There were private rooms, and just general out-of-control sucking and fucking. Then
Mayor Giuliani decided that adults weren't responsible to do what they wanted behind closed doors, and J's, along with most other hot spots in the city, became tame.

You can still get your rocks off here though, especially if it's 4am and the night hasn't treated you well. The door to the dungeon has a "Plenty Men Only" sign, as if women were just dying to get a taste of the action. The downstairs area is a cross between a bomb shelter and some leather queen's basement. There are pieces of S/M furniture lying around, left over from better days. One room has porno showing on a small TV on the far wall, with scattered chairs and benches. The other mostly empty room sees all the action. Lots of older guys, some tourists that have read about the place on the web, exhibitionists, younger guys coming from the Lure or Boots and Saddle

> "Men do not quit playing because they grow old; they grow old because they quit playing."
>
> **OLIVER WENDELL HOLMES**

or Dugout convene in the small, dank space, jerking each other off and watching each other jerk each other off. If you were lucky enough to participate in circle jerks as a kid, J's could bring back some beautiful memories. They don't serve alcohol here, so if you need to be drunk to engage in such debauchery, get liquored up before you come.

Upstairs there's always action at the pool table, dance music plays at a low level, and some pretty great porno gets guys in the mood if they're not already. New York Jacks, the oldest jackoff club in the country, meets here Monday and Thursday, and NY Bondage Club meets Friday. It's not what it used to be, but J's has survived the fascist administration, and provides a friendly atmosphere for ejaculation until the wee hours of the morning.

Your Words: "I've been coming here for years. There's something exciting about descending the stairs to the basement and curing what ails you." "Other people's penises are always fun."

SEX

Les Hommes

217B W 80th Street, 2nd Floor @ Broadway, Manhattan
Everyday 24 hours, 212.580.2445

Well, it's not Trump Tower or anything, but if you haven't found a mate at The Works or Candle Bar, Les Hommes is a hop, skip and hump away. There are video rooms with benches in the front and back, good for showing off your wares. About 15 booths with lockable doors line the right wall. Porno is playing in some booths. Inexplicably, professional wrestling and exercise videos play in others. At least it's a change of pace, but don't people get off from the real sex, rather than fake fighting? The attendant keeps an eye on the festivities.

Guys tend to be older, but since this is the only place of its kind in the area it attracts all types. Younger boys stop by in the afternoon and evening, and there's an after work influx of frustrated business types. Sometimes it's crowded; sometimes it's not. If not, be patient and don't waste your ten bucks. The front area has a small selection of new videos and a Mike Piazza poster on the door. The cashier is behind glass, along with lube, dildos and other videos. Maybe he is afraid of us. After you work up an appetite, go down the street and pick up an H & H bagel, the most delicious bagel to ever come out of New York. You'll feel doubly satisfied.

Your Words: "I live near Les Hommes, and as my hole needs pounding constantly..." "Not as classy as its French name, but it'll do."

Manhattan Sight and Sound

206 E 14th Street, 2nd Floor @ 3rd Avenue, Manhattan
Everyday 24 hours, 212.387.0596

Sometimes you just need to ejaculate, y'know? Manhattan Sight and Sound is conveniently located in the East Village and attracts myriad personalities. Tattooed love boys, older and younger Latino, black, and Italian men, horny businessmen, closet cases — they all roam the small corridors in the back of the second floor. Go in one of the 20-odd booths, preferably a booth next to one occupied by a boy you find attractive. Stick a minimum of five bucks in the slot, and stick your dick in the small glory hole, or vice versa. If you're lucky to have been referred to as "beercan" in the past, the fit's going to be tight. Of course you can just be a voyeur, or jack off to the porno. Don't forget tissues. Oh, and don't try to get away without paying — you will receive a loud, embarrassing knock on the

door. How romantic.

There's a decent porno selection in front, lots of it hetero, along with dildos, lube, etc. Downstairs there's a CD store, oddly enough, about the size of a small Sam Goody. After your brief affair upstairs, check it out. You might find a bargain. You probably won't find the love of your life here, but if you're having a frustrating day at the office or an unsuccessful night at the bars, come here and shoot a load.

Your Words: "I've sucked some fat dick here." "It's two blocks from my office. Thank God."

Unicorn All-Male Cinema

277C W 22nd Street, Between 7th & 8th Avenues, Manhattan
Everyday 24 hours, 212.924.2921

There's a small, juicy selection of videos and DVDs when you first walk into Unicorn, probably not how they make most of their money. For ten bucks, you walk through a turnstile in the back and enter Chelsea's only buddy booth meeting spot.

There are actually sofas situated around a TV when you first walk in the back. You can expect to watch different shows, sometimes marathons of Kids in the Hall. Watching Scott Thompson ramble on hilariously while boys are jerking each other off is pretty funny. Guys do watch the television and chat with each other. Behind the little rec room is a row of buddy booths, all playing a different porno flick. Eyes peek in and out looking for action. The atmosphere here is a bit more congenial than in similar semen-swapping places.

Head downstairs and the scent of rust and poppers washes over you. Fellows walk around the dark, dungeon-like basement ducking in and out of booths, and watching more pornos. There are little brick coves along the left wall that are almost oddly romantic. But generally it's grungy, seedy, and really fun if you're into it. We are in Chelsea, so the occasional impossible beauty does partake in the action. Generally, guys are in their twenties and thirties and are mostly gay, rather than straight and in denial. Unicorn is a few doors down from the popular bar Barracuda and isn't hurting for customers in the late hours.

Just walking around Chelsea can make you ravenous for flesh. Thankfully Unicorn All-Male Cinema is there to scratch the itch.

Your Words: "There should be 20 of these places in horny-ass Chelsea." "It scares me." "Good for a quick and convenient fix."

Wall Street Sauna

1 Maiden Lane @ Broadway, Manhattan
M-F 11am-8pm, Sa noon-midnight, Su noon-8pm, 212.233.8900

Owned by the same guys who bring you the East and West Side Clubs and the juicy 82nd Street Club, the Wall Street Sauna is smaller and a bit tamer than its sister sex locations. The place gets a bad rap in certain circles for its older clientele, but older guys need sex too, and can be just as hot and accommodating. Twelve bucks gains you entrance — no membership charges! The upstairs is pretty small, with about 50 rooms for getting off. Yeah, a lot of the guys are going gray, coming here from businesses around the area and hanging out before heading home for the evening, or getting off during their lunch break. Sex in the middle of the day makes for a productive afternoon. There's big screen porno when you first walk upstairs to get you going, but it's playing out in the open without seats surrounding the screen and feels odd. Go around the corner to your right and there's a row of around 15 rooms. This is the most secluded area and where a lot of the action happens.

Downstairs there's an open shower where well-endowed men show off their gifts while rubbing themselves down with Irish Spring. There's also a small sauna for chilling out. The staff is friendlier than in the other sex clubs, actually delivering a genuine smile while escorting you to your locker. If you find yourself feigning interest in a five hour meeting downtown, excuse yourself and head to Wall Street Sauna.

Your Words: "It's more relaxing and less pressure than similar places in the city." "How many years have I been coming here?" "The walls breathe sex."

West Side Club

27 W 20th Street, Between 5th & 6th Avenues, Manhattan
Everyday 24 hours, 212.691.2798

A sex club in Chelsea? Heavens to Betsy! Either this idea thrills or repulses you. Well, even though Chelsea has a reputation for muscle clone attitude, if you're patient and assertive (not pushy or overbearing, just a little assertive), you'll eventually find what you're looking for here no matter who you are or where you're from.

It's no accident that this is the only sex club with a gym. This place actually used to be an aerobics studio, so maybe healthy vibes are in the air. West Side does attract boys that look like they've stepped out of a magazine ad. Often, there's actually a line to get in late on weekend nights, as beautiful men from Barracuda, G and the clubs end up here for a nightcap. If you go earlier rather than later, you're liable to find more of a variety of guys. If you're a man with abs to die for and pecs that stop a clock, then take your pick and fuck 'til the cows come home! There are around 100 rooms, a sauna, a steam room, showers, and that gym. Some find the staff members rude; others swear they're friendly. It matters how you interact with them, and what stage the moon is in that night.

You can either purchase a temporary pass that allows you five entries, or an annual membership. Pay for either a room or just a locker. The room might be worth an investment — you don't want to risk being left out in the cold with your newfound friend. It wouldn't hurt to bring your favorite condom and lube. Take off your clothes, put on your towel, and get laid.

Your Words: "About a million times better than sitting at home and jerking off to pornos." "I actually met my boyfriend here. Love can be found in the seediest of places."

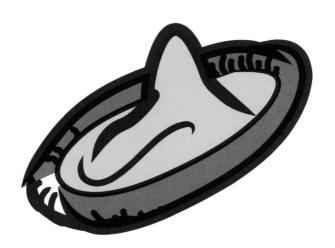

Community

▼

Maybe the best thing about being queer in this day and age is that you automatically become part of a growing, caring community. No matter where you live, there are clubs, bookstores, organizations and support groups to enhance your life. New York City is home to the largest population of lesbian, gay, bisexual and transgender folk in the country, and we are outspoken, encouraging, and diverse. If you're new to the city or have just come out and feel overwhelmed by the options, the Gay and Lesbian Community Services Center is a great place to start learning about what's available. They provide periodic orientation programs to familiarize neophyte queers with our bustling queer city. It is the location for hundreds of clubs and support groups, and their schedule is listed on their website or at the Center on a daily basis. A book on all the New York queer community has to offer would encompass volumes; the following section is designed to present a representative example of lesbian and gay organizations. Most have been around for many years, and have a proven track record of providing the populace with unique and valuable resources. You are never alone. The opportunity for learning and giving increases with each passing day.

ACT UP

Lesbian and Gay Community Center
1 Little West 12th Street @ Gansevoort Street, Manhattan
General Meetings: M 7:30pm, 212.996.4783
www.actupny.org

The practice and results of civil disobedience seem like a thing of the past for us jaded 21st century cynics. Yet for about 15 years, through non-violent protest ACT UP has been instrumental in ensuring human rights for people living with AIDS and HIV. Unlike the politicians and pharmaceutical companies that hold the most power in preventing the disease and taking steps to find a cure, the members of ACT UP deal directly with the disease every day and look for the most direct actions to end the plague. The group fights for valuable needle exchange programs, fights to end 'names reporting' of people that test positive to government health departments, works with federal organizations to allow the use of experimental drugs in the U.S, and draws attention to international AIDS issues.

ACT UP members march, shout, interrupt, report, monitor, disseminate and educate. Their meetings and website are probably the best way to find out the latest developments concerning HIV and AIDS. Did you know George Dubya didn't once say the word "AIDS" publicly during his tenure as governor of Texas, even though that state has the fourth-highest number of AIDS cases in the U.S.? Do you know why affordable medications aren't available in Africa, where millions of people have already died? Come to a meeting and find out, or check out their website. Donate some money or buy some merchandise. The plague is far from over. We are not silent.

Bluestockings Women's Bookstore

172 Allen Street @ Stanton Street, Manhattan
Tu-Su noon-8pm, 212.777.6028

This bookstore is a godsend. It's the rare retail location that exists purely for altruistic reasons. Planning to incorporate as a non-profit in the near future, Bluestockings is a true collective, primarily run by volunteers. The atmosphere is conducive to spending hours sifting through books you can't find anywhere else, and interacting with other women from the five boroughs.

The store is small and comfortably informal. Chairs and tables are spread throughout the store inviting you to stay awhile, even though space is precious. Sharing the corner with the art section is a little stage that hosts some big talent. Notable authors and musicians often choose Bluestockings for readings and performances over the larger bookstores in the area. Events take place three or four times a week, and include acoustic open mics, movie screenings, and unconventional readings.

The book selection is focused and distinct. Bluestockings carries self-published titles and hard-to-find fanzines, as well as major and small publishers of lesbian fiction, cultural studies, queer theory and self-improvement. Volunteer recommendation cards stick out of displayed books, attracting customers to leftfield titles. For example, a Disney young adult series called Cheetah Girls was recommended for its powerful role models. Who knew? And what other bookstore has Book of Choices: New York Resources For Unplanned Pregnancy featured on their table? They also will go out of their way to fill special orders. An eclectic collection

COMMUNITY

of accessories is sold here — pick up Dyke TV videos, a Keeper Reusable Menstrual Cup, or Backdoor Boys undies. The CD selection is small, but prices are usually three or four bucks lower than anywhere else. A small café serves delicious lattes and delectable treats like Almond Butter Brownies.

The name "bluestocking" comes from an 18th century British term meaning "a woman with strong or scholarly or literary interests." Bluestockings successfully fulfills the scholarly, literary and entertainment needs of New York's lesbian and general female communities, and serves as a valuable resource to residents and tourists alike.

Your Words: "Vastly different from any bookstore in the city. The staff is knowledgeable and the events are unique and fun." "Going to a discussion group or an open mic here beats going to a bar or staying home and watching TV."

Creative Visions Bookstore

548 Hudson Street, Between Perry & Charles Streets, Manhattan
Su-Th noon-10pm, F-Sa noon-11pm, 212.645.7573

In the age of daunting superstores and Amazon-sized websites, many local, community-based bookstores have fallen by the wayside. Thankfully, Creative Visions has been thriving on peaceful Hudson St. since 1985, and serves as a valuable resource for the queer community of New York. The store is smaller than Barnes & Noble's fiction section, but boasts a wide selection of gay and lesbian literature, raunchy videos and more.

Creative Visions has mostly every queer publication in print, including all the Dykes to Watch Out For titles, fiction from Nathan Aldyne to Edmund White, a large self-improvement section, every gay travel book you could think of (Gay Guide to Africa!), periodicals like On Our Backs and Handjobs, and old copies of Cherry Tales dating back to the 80's. Near the old porno mags is an amazing collection of old porno photographs for the retro masturbator — pictures of groovy 70's mustached men pleasuring themselves for the camera, sailors, mothers, bodybuilders, drag queens, etc. They also are home to a huge video collection with over 7000 titles. Covers are neatly organized by price in loose-leaf binders. Take home Bronx Boys for $4, Men of Lake Michigan for $3, or Depth Charge for $2. If you can't find Relax It's Just Sex or Priest on DVD at your local video palace, they have it here. You'll find greeting cards for every occasion throughout the store, and if you're picking up a present for someone, the staff will wrap it free of charge.

Bookstores are great places to chill out for an hour or two, and Visions creates a pleasant atmosphere for shopping. Pictures of pride marches, Quentin Crisp, and stills from Boys Don't Cry line the walls. Classical music plays low, and even though the store is small, there's enough space to feel comfortable. There's always a clerk perched near the entrance for questions and recommendations. They also welcome phone and email orders. Locally owned and operated, Creative Visions is a great stop for a good read.

Your Words: "The best, cheapest place to get a porno." "There're lots of little gems on quiet Hudson St. — this is one of them."

Crossdressers International

Call for meeting times, 212.570.7389
members.tripod.com/CDINYC

Whether you identify as a transsexual, transvestite, or even if you identify as a firefighter but love to wear panties, blouses and a bra around the house — Crossdressers International provides an opportunity to meet like-minded gender benders and have a good time. Trade makeup tips, give and get advice on relationships, and socialize in the garb that makes you feel most comfortable.

Society beats up on men that are brave enough to

show
their feminine
side (and vice versa, for
that matter). Crossdressers creates a
safe atmosphere for members to be themselves.
They can get a key to the CDI apartment, leave their
"day clothes" there, change into their fabulous outfits,
and are free to roam the city as a woman without lug-
ging their other clothes in a backpack. Not that there's
any pressure to roam the city as the opposite gender.
Some members just come for the events — fashion
shows, makeup demos, wine tasting, discussions, etc.

The CDI website features pictures of many members
including the proud founder, a list of places where crossdressers hang out, and a membership application.
Regular meetings are held Thursday and an Open House
is held each Wednesday. To all those crossdressers who

haven't worn their favorite wig out of the house — stop hiding your flair for fashion and head over to a CDI meeting.

Date Bait

Call for meeting times & locations, 212.971.1084
www.datebait.com

People don't date enough anymore. Lately it seems either you're single and bitter, or in a long-term relationship, and there's no in-between. For people who are sick of dealing with slobbering, drunk suitors at bars, paying large sums of cash to dating services, or finding out your online dreamboat is actually married and the wrong gender to boot — Date Bait to the rescue.

There are lesbian, gay men, and straight events. Gay male and straight events happen about two or three times a month, and lesbian events about once every two months. You walk in, pay 15 bucks, and get an ID number. If you're early, you might as well start chatting, since everybody's looking anyway and would love to talk instead of stewing in their anxiety. Then everyone takes turns speaking about themselves for one minute. Unless you're an experienced extemporaneous orator, take an index card up with you or have something rehearsed. Don't worry if you mess up — vulnerability is cute. After the show, there's a mingling period of 30 minutes in which you get to know your potential dates better. Then hand in your computer card with the ID number of each person you want to eventually see naked, and wait for the results.

If you pick someone and they pick you — well, how about that! Looks like you got yourself a date. Some lucky dogs get many matches; some poor souls get none. If you're a poor soul, don't worry — the founder of Date Bait didn't get matched his first time out either. Next time you find yourself eating a frozen meal while watching Suddenly Susan reruns and feeling sorry for yourself, find out when the next Date Bait is being held, and start

COMMUNITY

rehearsing your exciting self-description. You never know.

Dignity/NY

Call for meeting times and locations, 212.627.6488
www.dignityny.org

Dignity/NY is part of Dignity/USA, the largest and most active group of lesbian, gay, bisexual, and transgender Catholics. Being gay and Catholic may seem mutually exclusive to some, but there are many members of the Catholic community that disagree with the homophobic dogma of the current Catholic Church, and make an effort to bridge the gap. Dignity provides a home for these free thinkers.

The backbone and purpose of Dignity is to encourage a vital community life through volunteer outreach, social activities and non-violent protest. A Pastoral Care program is currently in development, with the goal of providing support to the elderly, ill, and emotionally disturbed members of their congregations. Also active politically, members of Dignity meet with lawmakers to discuss non-discrimination issues. They've sued the City of New York for permission to demonstrate in front of St. Patrick's Cathedral, and as

far back as 1974, they helped organize city clergy in support of a gay civil rights law. They also subsidized the first known religiously sponsored AIDS ministry in the U.S. Since 1972, Dignity has demonstrated their faith with action and benevolence.

Often when lesbians and gays separate from their family or hometown, they disconnect from their faith also. Dignity provides the opportunity for Catholics to reaffirm their spirituality through liturgy, public service and community.

Front Runners

Call for meeting times and locations, 212.724.9700
www.frontrunnersnewyork.com

Find yourself running out of steam lately? Is your job running your life? Put on your sneaks and have fun with Front Runners. Running is a great way to clear your head and to see different parts of New York, and the Front Runners provide a non-competitive, supportive atmosphere to tackle the city in stride.

For beginners and recreational runners, Front Runners organizes two weekly fun runs in Manhattan and one in Brooklyn, and often schedule "special runs" in out of the way locations. For the more serious runner, Front Runners puts together teams for the world famous New York City Marathon and the New York Triathlon, sponsors an indoor track meet, and has established a coaching and training program to help members reach their fitness goals. For competitive types, their website provides info on all the races in the tri-state area. The website is updated frequently, and provides links to other related clubs and races around town.

What better way to demonstrate pride than running like a gazelle? Front Runners sponsors the Lesbian and Gay Pride Run every June. Putting aside some time for fun, the group travels to Philadelphia, Boston and D.C running events, and plans excursions to Broadway shows, restaurants and Gay Men's Chorus performances.

COMMUNITY

So stretch those muscles, put on that cute tank top that's been hiding in the back of your closet, and go running.

Gay and Lesbian Alliance Against Defamation

248 West 35th Street, 8th Floor, Between 7th & 8th Avenues, Manhattan, 212.629.3322, www.glaad.org

GLAAD was formed in New York in 1985 and began their work by protesting the conservative New York Post's offensive coverage of the AIDS crisis. When we think of media intervention and protest, high-profile conflicts such as Dr. Laura's slanderous speech and Andy Rooney's hateful words come to mind, but some of the victories GLAAD has helped win over the years aren't as well known but just as meaningful. In 1989, they worked with Daily Variety in reversing their policy against listing survivors of same-sex couples in obituaries. In 1997, they organized a live broadcast of the "Ellen" coming out show in Birmingham after the local ABC affiliate refused to air the show. This combination of grass roots

organizing across the country and working with media creators in homophobic Hollywood has made GLAAD one of the most influential political action groups currently operating, queer or otherwise.

Many Americans "interact" with television characters more than live human beings on a daily basis. Television, film and popular music are thought of as harmless entertainment, but 1000s of hours of watching and listening over a course of a lifetime have an effect on individual and global consciousness. GLAAD realized the importance of positive lesbian and gay imagery in the media. If you grew up in the 70s or 80s, the gay and lesbian images you were exposed to on TV were Jack Tripper faking homosexuality to reside with buxom girls, or Eddie Murphy saying "I'm afraid of gay people" on HBO. Things have changed over the years. GLAAD has worked with TV shows and movies to actually re-edit scenes that convey homophobia.

GLAAD mobilizes large volunteer teams across the country to acts as liaisons to local press and media, lobby politicians, and demonstrate and rally against injustice. Check out the website or give them a call if you want to participate or donate.

Gay and Lesbian Community Services Center

One Little West 12th Street @ Gansevoort Street, Manhattan
Everyday 9am-11pm, 212.620.7310

Whether you're vacationing in the city or have lived here all your life, the Center provides endless opportunities for personal growth, meeting friends, and helping others. In operation for almost 20 years, the Center caters to every interest and need imaginable. Where else do Armenian, Irish, Puerto Rican, Japanese, Polish and African organizations

> "You and me together, fighting for our love?"
>
> **BRONSKI BEAT**
> *Why*

meet under the same roof? The Center holds discussion groups for the polyamorous, provides support for breast cancer survivors, encourages spiritual development through bible study, Eckankar teachings, and meditation, and fosters creativity through workshops and performance.

Successful long term projects that the center has undertaken include: Center Global Action network, an international gay and lesbian rights program, CenterBridge, an AIDS bereavement program, and Center Kids, a family project. A wide variety of weekly special events offer career advice, provide networking opportunities, and instruct on subjects ranging from Israeli folk dance to psychic ability. An "Immigrant Orientation" is held periodically for people new to the City, or just coming out. The best way to find out what's going on there is through their website, which is updated daily.

One of the many benefits to being lesbian and gay in the 21st century is no matter where you go, there are others with common interests and backgrounds to exchange ideas, lend a helping hand, or to just have fun. You are never alone. The Lesbian and Gay Community Services Center is maybe the world's best example of a concentrated, organized queer community. Next time you're glued to the television or utter the words "I'm bored" or "I'm lonely," head over to the Center and experience life.

Your Words: "I wrote my first play at the Center." "A great alternative to running from bar to bar." "It always amazes me every time I look at the daily event listing — there's always something going on that interests me."

> "The Pledge of Allegiance says, 'With liberty and justice for all.' What part of all don't you understand?"
>
> **REP. PAT SCHROEDER**

Gay Male S/M Activists

Call for meeting times and locations, 212.727.9878
www.gmsma.org

GMSMA is an intelligent organization, promoting safety, education and good old S/M fun. Their purpose is to help create a more supportive S/M community for gay men, whether they are new to the scene or have been practicing for years. They emphasize responsibility, tradition, and discuss the medical and technical aspects of S/M.

The topics of their periodic programs are more engaging and creative than the subject matter of most other organizations' meetings. Past discussions include: The Doctor Is In — education on how to handle an S/M injury; The Biker Mystique — examining the power of the biker myth; Switch Hitting — about men who alternate between top and bottom roles; and Things That Pinch — I'll leave that to your imagination. Past seminars include Candles and Hot Wax, The Art of the Boot Black, Fire Play, Steel Bondage, and Electricity. And then there are great articles in their newsletters — "Barbershop Scenes," "Observations on Fisting," "Spending a Night in the Doghouse" and "What's the Big Deal About

Spanking Butts?" You get the idea.

If the above topics interest you, go ahead and fill out a membership form on the website. At the very least, if you're interest is piqued, check out the newsletter articles also on their site. Be safe and have a ball.

Gay Men's Health Crisis

119 West 24th Street, Between 6th & 7th Avenues, Manhattan
M-F 11am-8pm; Hotline M-F 10am-9pm, Sa noon-3pm
212.807.6655, www.gmhc.org

In July 1981, a New York Times article alerted the world to a "Rare Cancer Seen in 41 Homosexuals." In response to the new crisis, 80 men met in Larry Kramer's apartment to hear him speak about "gay cancer." The group pooled together over $6,000 for medical research, and six months later founded Gay Men's Health Crisis. A year later, the world's first AIDS hotline on the answering machine of a dedicated volunteer received 100 calls a night. GHMC thus began its unwavering commitment to caring for people with AIDS, and affecting treatment and prevention of the disease.

GHMC aids over 11,000 clients yearly, and employs over 6,600 volunteers and more than 169 staff. They provide legal assistance, help individuals obtain government insurance and benefits, treat patients with HIV and AIDS, and test the general population for the disease. Volunteers work directly with clients, offer legal help, run

workshops, offer administrative help, assist with
fundraising, and fulfill other needs. GMHC also
encourages the public to lobby their government rep-
resentatives, and write opinion pieces in local magazines and newspapers.

For over two decades, GMHC has fought long and
hard to help people living with AIDS, and will continue to do so with our support.

Lavender Light

70A Greenwich Avenue #315 @ 7th Avenue, Manhattan
212.714.7072, www.lavenderlight.com

The 50 or so members of Lavender Light are people
of all colors and come from all backgrounds, but all
are gay and lesbian identified, and all love to sing.
They inspire audiences every time they perform, lift-
ing every single soul out of its seat. The vocal and
musical arrangements are unique, and the solo and
collective voices are strong and soaring. Not just
anyone can join — auditions are stringent. The
result is an amazing collection of gay and lesbian
talent.

Their musical selection encompasses classic and
contemporary gospel, new arrangements of pop
songs, and original work. They've performed on the
public television gem "In the Life," the People of
Color Joint Kwanzaa Ceremony and held their Spring
Concert at the prestigious Town Hall. They've
released two CDs to critical acclaim, Lavender Light,
which made it to #1 on The Advocate's list of favorite
CDs, and Light in the House, recorded live in 2000
and successfully capturing the spiritual energy. They
are worth seeking out! They've performed at Alice
Tully Hall, Carnegie Hall, the Brooklyn Academy of
Music, and hopefully they're performing near you
soon. Check out their website for details, or buy their
CD at one of the bookstores listed in this book.
Rejoice!

COMMUNITY

Lesbian Herstory Archives

Address and office hours available with appointment
718.768.DYKE, www.lesbianherstoryarchives.org

During the 20th Century, lesbian and gay people formed visible, thriving communities. We made history. Who's recording our accomplishments for future generations? The Lesbian Herstory Archives collects and preserves books, magazines, journals, news clippings, poetry and prose, posters, and all forms of media relevant to the lives and actions of lesbians around the world. A visit to their Park Slope location is an eye-opening, unparalleled learning experience.

In 1974, the archives opened in the pantry of Joan Nestle's and Deborah Edel's Upper West Side apartment, utilizing materials collected over the years. Pretty soon the collection started taking over the space, and the coordinators created a slide show to spread the word about the archives. Over 25 years later, the Archives house over 20,000 volumes, 12,000 photographs, 300 special collections, and much more.

Although nothing can substitute a visit to their site,

the Archives answers reference requests from around the world. As you can imagine, the task of gathering and organizing the vast amount of material is enormous. They're always looking for volunteers to help out, and for donations. Please call ahead of time for an appointment if you plan to visit. Whether researching for a specific project or browsing for your own personal education, a trip to the Lesbian Herstory Archives is valuable and unforgettable.

Michael Callen-Audrey Lorde Community Health Center

356 West 18th Street, Between 8th & 9th Avenues, Manhattan
212.271.7200, www.callen-lorde.org

In an age where HMO's treat patients like fast food customers, Callen-Lorde Community Health Center provides quality care while treating patients with compassion and intelligence. Michael Callen was a colorful, talented AIDS activist who died in 1993; Audre Lorde was a New York State poet laureate, feminist, and long-time survivor of breast center. Honoring their memory, Callen-Lorde is a merciful organization, meeting the health care needs of our community regardless of any patient's ability to pay. They are New York's only medical facility dedicated to meeting the needs of the LGBT community.

Primary Care at Callen-Lorde includes lesbian, HIV/AIDS, transgender, and senior services, in addition to outreach for teens. Their social services division offers counseling, case management and support group services. Their Health Education Resource Center (HERC) is open to members of the general public, and has trained volunteers to help access accurate, reliable health information.

Formerly the Community Health Project (CHP), Callen-Lorde recently relocated to a larger facility in Chelsea, and last year treated over 27,000. The LGBT community often encounters homophobia in medical

COMMUNITY

settings, whether it's outright discrimination or ignorance of issues concerning us. Many are too intimidated or uncomfortable to seek out treatment or advice. Callen-Lorde succeeds in providing a safe haven for us, and already has met its goal of improving the health of our community.

New York Gay & Lesbian Anti-Violence Project

240 West 35th Street, Between 7th & 8th Avenues, Manhattan
212.714.1184, www.avp.org

AVP was founded in 1980 in reaction to incidents of anti-gay violence and the failure of the criminal justice system to respond. Twenty years later, reported incidents of violence are still on the rise. We suffer physical and verbal abuse by police, service providers, and coworkers. AVP provides free and confidential services to victims and others affected by violence, helping them to evaluate their options and assert their rights.

The Project works to educate the public, law enforcement officials and social service agencies about violence directed at our community. A good example is the Safe Bar project. Pick-up crimes account for over 13 percent of the Project's non-domestic violence cases, and violent acts from strangers often occur near known gay hangouts. Drawing participation from bartenders and bar managers, AVP raises the visibility of hate-motivated violence, pick-up crimes and domestic violence that occurs in or near bars. The agency also maintains a 24-hour crisis intervention hotline staffed by professional counselors and trained volunteers. Victims are often afraid to go to the "authorities," and the hotline provides an easy avenue for reporting and dealing with violence. AVP also keeps the media abreast on issues of anti-gay violence through press releases and study reports.

In the wake of the Matthew Shepherd tragedy, consciousness has been raised concerning the issue of anti-queer violence. Sadly, the problems still pervade. Thankfully, AVP is helping victims rebuild their lives and working to prevent further tragedies from taking place.

Oscar Wilde Bookshop

15 Christopher Street, Between 6th & 7th Avenues, Manhattan
M-Sa 11am-8pm, Su noon-7pm, 212.255.8097

Billed as the "World's Oldest Gay & Lesbian Bookshop," Oscar Wilde Bookshop opened in 1967 and was initially subject to bomb threats, smashed windows, and scrawled obscenities. According to Martin Duberman in the book Stonewall, the staff of the bookshop served as a "counseling agency for more than a thousand young homosexual men and women." Luckily for NY queers, the bookstore still thrives today.

Oscar Wilde Bookshop might be the cleanest, most organized bookstore in the city. The space is small and has the potential of being cramped and unruly like many independent bookstores, but every section is impeccably organized. Even the used books section, usually an eyesore in most shops, is alphabetized.

The range in many gay and lesbian bookshops across the country strongly leans toward one gender or the other. Impressively, OWB serves both communities equally and comprehensively. There are separate male and female mystery sections, and the knick-knacks, ranging from Marky Mark light switch plates to Marcie and Peppermint Patty lesbian T-shirts to rainbow boas, cover all bases. Overall, the book selection is smart and somewhat diverse for a small queer bookstore. Stylish titles like Pad the Guide to Ultra Living and Wizard of Oz Pop-Up Book appeal to people of all orientations. The fiction and biography sections are complete and demonstrate knowledge on the part of the staff. There are also unique, hard-to-find artifacts for sale, including autographed George Gershwin and W. Somerset Maugham photographs. And where else

COMMUNITY

could you find a stack of Importance of Being Earnest comic books?

There's also a decent selection of CDs and DVDs toward the front. Lots of mainstream stuff, although they sell a gay rap group CD — Rainbow Flava! Although they do carry erotica titles, Oscar doesn't rely on the flesh for appeal. The staff is helpful and unobtrusive. Oscar would be proud.

Your Words: "One of many super bookstores in the area." "The books they choose to display are always intriguing."

PFLAG

Parents, Families and Friends of Lesbians and Gays
110 14th Street, NW, Suite 1030
Washington, DC 20005
202.638.4200, www.pflag.org/pflag.html

As many of us know, it can be extraordinarily difficult for lesbian and gay individuals to come out to family and friends. Growing up, we learn to hide our orientation from ourselves and the people we love. It can be just as difficult for our family and friends, who have been raised in the same homophobic atmosphere that we have to come to terms with our sexuality and lifestyle. The mission of PFLAG is to promote the health of LBGT individuals, support and educate their families and friends, to enlighten an ill-informed public, and to serve as an advocate to end discrimination and to secure equal rights.

The PFLAG booklets provided on their website illustrate how the organization stimulates communication and understanding. "Is Homosexuality a Sin?" consults religious experts about questions concerning families and friends of gays and lesbians. "Be Yourself" reaches out to teenagers who are suffering by understanding their feelings in the face of adversity. "Our Daughters and Sons" asks the question "What do you do when you find out that your child is gay, lesbian or bisexual?" and counsels by helping to answer other questions that arise when dealing with the revelation. These topics are indicative of the subject matter covered in meetings held by more than 450 affiliates worldwide.

PLAG also acts as a resource for schools, politicians, journalists, and businesses. Their message is widespread. Betty Degeneres, parent of the pioneer Ellen Degeneres, has said, "There are no exceptions to unconditional love." Thanks to PFLAG, that message is heard every day in diverse communities across the nation.

Pride Senior Network

356 West 18th Street, Between 8th & 9th Avenues, Manhattan
212.271.7288, www.pridesenior.org

As lesbian and gay men and women grow older, they face the issues other senior citizens face, but with twists. What legal documents need to be obtained to ensure that a significant other can oversee medical care and financial concerns? What health care providers are gay and lesbian sensitive? What retirement homes can cater to gay and lesbian needs? The Pride Senior Network aims to educate seniors about their options.

For a low $10 membership fee, seniors have access to: a directory of services providing details and consumer information about providers, and a newsletter with articles covering issues from fitness to finance. The resource directory includes services offering a welcoming and affirmative attitude toward the LGBT senior population. As the government is withdrawing services for the aging even as the elderly population increases, PSN also acts as an advocate for seniors.

More than 75,000 gays and lesbians over 65 live in New York City. Since the LGBT culture is unfairly

COMMUNITY

focused on youth, the aging population can feel invisible. PSN is a young organization hoping to offer a full range network of services for the "invisible" population. Judging by their progress thus far, it looks like they will succeed.

Lodging

NYC hotel rates can be exorbitant. For the price of a weekend in some Midtown hotels, you could pay rent for a year. The irony is that when visiting New York, the last place you want to be is holed up in some hotel. There's too much to see and do! In case you don't have rich friends putting you up in the guest room, the next section provides inexpensive alternatives to the big chain hotels. Privately owned bed and breakfasts and guest houses often reflect the personality of the owners, and provide a fun change to the homogenous décor of large hotels. All lodging options listed are gay owned and operated, or gay friendly. Most have polite, informed staff members ready to aid you in your exploration of New York. Make sure to check out each location's website to help you make your decision. Here's to a pleasant stay and a good night's sleep.

333 West 88th Associates

333 W 88th Street, Between West End Avenue & Riverside Drive, Manhattan, 212.724.9818, www.333w88.com

Don't be fooled by the corporate-sounding name — 333 West 88th Associates is a restored limestone brownstone on the Upper West Side. Each room has its own separate apartment and features numerous amenities including: a networked, fully functional PC and printer, VCR, stereo system, answering machine, feather/down comforter in the winter and cotton blankets in the summer, a kitchen with microwave oven, stove, refrigerator and coffee maker — all at no additional charge. Some rooms have a futon or a roll away bed for extra guests. One room even features a working chord organ. What else could you want for such an inexpensive rate?

There are no non-smoking rooms as 333 hosts many international guests that smoke, but rooms are consistently aired out, and have blinds rather than curtains so that they don't absorb smoke. The staff is beyond helpful and accommodating, and the service alone draws guests back repeatedly. The website has detailed descriptions and pictures of each room, helping the customer choose between a budget or luxury unit. 333 West 88th offers privacy, lots of space, and great service for an inexpensive rate.

Your Words: "Simply decorated, and really, really cheap." "The gregarious staff makes me feel right at home."

Abingdon Guest House

13 8th Avenue, Between W 12th & Jane Street, Manhattan 212.243.5384, www.abingdonguesthouse.com

While a lot of bed and breakfasts in the area have a modest, somewhat homogenous décor, Abingdon goes the extra mile. Each room is distinctive and tasteful. The Garden Room features exposed brick and a working fireplace, as do many of the rooms. The red walls in the Ambassador

Room are striking. The Martinique Room houses a gorgeous canopy bed, and the Essex Room day bed makes you want to lay down and curl up with a good book. Pictures of the rooms can be seen on their website.

All rooms have private baths, located within the rooms or adjacent to them. Amenities include in-room safes, bathrobes, and air conditioning. Some rooms have a view of the patio garden. Although it's located a few blocks from rowdy Christopher Street, Abingdon is in a quiet, charming area of the West Village. It's perfect for a romantic getaway.

Your Words: "The rooms are amazing. I can't believe they don't charge more." "A peaceful respite from the hectic city."

> **"In my lifetime, I've been to bed with men, women, and odd pieces of furniture."**
>
> **TALLULAH BANKHEAD**

Chelsea Inn

46 W 17th Street, Between 5th & 6th Avenues, Manhattan, 212.645.8989, www.chelseainn.com

Chelsea Inn is quirky, cheap and comfy. Not as homey as some of the other guesthouses in the area, the Inn does have its benefits. For one, there are internet bargain specials, running as low as $89, an almost unheard of price for New York City lodging. A guest room with a shared bath starts at $109, and a studio with a private bath starts at $139.

And then there are the bathrooms. Murals and abstract designs were painted by art students from Yale and Parsons School of Design. The effect is striking and pleasing, and suggests the impression of an expensive foreign hotel. The furniture in each room is equally unusual — mismatched and random but cool. The rooms are pretty large and the suites even larger. The kitchenettes make it easy for the traveler on a budget to save some dough. Security is adequate; there are in-room safes, the front door is locked every night, and only Inn guests are

LODGING

allowed entry. Most rooms are away from the street and pretty quiet. Chelsea Inn is located in the up-and-coming Flatiron District, and surrounded by hundreds of restaurants and attractions. As inexpensive as you're going to get for staying in New York, Chelsea Inn is a great choice for the budget minded.

Your Words: "When I go to NY, I like to save my money for the food and the clubs. The cheap rates at Chelsea Inn allow me to do that." "The bathrooms are surreal. They're good for taking a bath and writing in your journal."

Chelsea Mews Guesthouse

344 W 15th Street, Between 8th & 9th Avenues, Manhattan
212.255.9174

If you love visiting New York City but occasionally the chaos and noise of the city gets to you, Chelsea Mews Guesthouse may be your haven away from home. Chelsea Mews is a quiet, unassuming guesthouse on a quiet, unassuming block across from St. Vincent's hospital in Chelsea. The building has been a gay lodging operation since 1941. Once upon a time there was an antique store on the premises, and some of the furniture from the store decorates the rooms. There's definitely a sense of history to the place, especially if you chat with the owner. There are nine rooms, some with private baths. The rooms with single beds are pretty small, and the double bedrooms vary in size. TV, air conditioning and maid services are

available. If you ever wanted to sit on a NYC stoop and meditate with the sounds of the city, you can do it here. The parking situation on the street is a bit better than other spots in the neighborhood. The innkeeper is forever making renovations and looking after things, but otherwise you may not see anybody else in the house during your visit. Simple, peaceful and cheap, Chelsea Mews is a mellow place to stay in a hopping, vibrant neighborhood.

Your Words: "A little oasis in the middle of Chelsea." "Cozy and quaint."

Chelsea Pines Inn

317 W 14th Street, Between 8th & 9th Avenues, Manhattan
212.929.1023, www.chelseapinesinn.com

More modern in tone than some of the other gay lodging options in the area, Chelsea Pines Inn is fun and friendly. Each room is named after an old film star, some famous and some forgotten. Founder Sheldon Post said he tried to resist creating a Judy Garland, but it was inevitable. The room features the biggest poster of A Child Is Waiting you'll ever see. Most rooms are decently sized, especially for the prices. Some have private bathrooms — the ones that don't have private showers.

In the morning, the staff serves homemade bread and Krispy Kreme doughnuts to their guests. There's no better way to start the day with a melt-in-your-mouth Krispy Kreme. The breakfast nook in the back leads to a small, charming garden with chairs for lounging. The location is convenient to both the Village and Chelsea, and the staff will be more than happy to help you get around with directions and suggestions.

Chelsea Pines Inn has been honored by the gay travel publication Out and About for consecutive years, and consistently receives high marks from other travel publications. When you don't want to spend an arm and a leg when visiting New York, Chelsea Pines Inn is a marvelous option.

Your Words: "Comfortable and festive." "The friendly staff sets the tone."

Chelsea Savoy Hotel

204 W 23rd Street, Between 8th & 9th Avenues, Manhattan
212.929.9353, www.chelseasavoy.citysearch.com

The text on the home page of the Chelsea Savoy Hotel website begins with the sentence, "The Chelsea Savoy Hotel rises high above its rivals." Damn, them's fightin' words! I guess this isn't your average little homey place to stay. Actually, the Chelsea Savoy is a modern structure built from the ground up, in contrast to many other hotels in the city that have been converted from old buildings. The rooms are furnished with all the amenities — large desks in case you're forced to work on holidays, mini-fridges, goose-down pillows, individual room climate control, and specially designed rooms for disabled folk. The rooms are like chain hotel rooms, but without the chain hotel prices. A single room for 100 bucks in this city is hard to come by.

Chelsea Savoy is a good reflection of the surrounding queer neighborhood. It's young, brash, clean and confident. Dance music pumps in the lobby. The front desk staff, youthful and cute, is adequate but not overly friendly. The location is conveniently located next to the 8th Avenue subway line, and very near all the Chelsea hotspots. If you stumble home from the bars and clubs that the area has to offer, Chelsea Savoy is a great place to crash at 4am. Chelsea Savoy is a welcome addition to the neighborhood.

Your Words: "I can't believe the prices are this low. You would pay double the amount in Midtown for the same quality." "An amazing bargain in a city that drains your bank account."

> "Home was anywhere with diesel gas, love was a trucker's hand. Never stuck around long enough for a one-night stand."

MAGNETIC FIELDS
Papa Was a Rodeo

Colonial House Inn

318 W 22nd Street, Between 8th & 9th Avenues, Manhattan
212.243.9669, www.colonialhouseinn.com

Before he converted it into an award-winning bed and breakfast, Mel Cheren, owner of the Colonial House Inn on West 22nd Street, used to donate rooms in his building to the Gay Men's Health Crisis. Eventually GMHC outgrew the space, and Cheren renovated the 1850's structure in order to transform the building into a guesthouse. Back in the 70s, Cheren was also owner of the pioneering disco club Paradise Garage, and is the author of the popular book My Life at the Paradise Garage. You'll hear no Sylvester or Donna Summer here; instead, Cheren now provides a simple, inexpensive lodging option for gay travelers.

If you're visiting during the warmer months, the roofdeck, with a "clothing optional" area, is a pleasing amenity, especially in an area with few spots for relaxing outside. Colonial House serves breakfast every morning, served in the lounge near the entrance. Rooms are furnished with soft colored, abstract artwork, and include air conditioning, and washing facilities. The staff is always accommodating. Colonial House is an exceptional choice for the budget conscious, queer globetrotter.

Your Words: "I always stay here when I'm in New York — two words: the roof!" "The staff is professional and fun."

Country Inn The City

270 W 77th Street, Between Broadway & West End Avenue,
Manhattan, 212.580.4183, www.countryinnthecity.com

New Yorkers that don't make more than 75K a year often find themselves in a studio apartment smaller than the room that they slept in when they were 12. Unfortunately for visitors to the Big Apple, accommodations can be equally claustrophobic. If you need some space for stretching out but don't want to spend half your salary,

Country
Inn the City is a
viable lodging option.

The Inn offers a full 550
square feet of living space, including
queen-sized beds, well-equipped kitchenettes,
answering machines, and air conditioning. The bathrooms are spacious and full of amenities. The interior of
each apartment is impeccably detailed and gorgeous.
Light pours through windows in each room. All bedding
is hypoallergenic and the mattresses are comfy.

The neighborhood is nothing to sneeze at either.

Most residents would consider themselves extremely lucky to live on the Upper West Side, amidst gourmet groceries, quirky shops, and walking distance from Museum of Natural History, Lincoln Center, and Central Park. It isn't a gay neighborhood, per se, but there's a queer presence here, as there is in most Manhattan neighborhoods. Prices are reasonable, but be sure to check out the Last Minute Specials link on the website for possible extra bargains. Country Inn the City definitely provides the chance to live life in high New York style for a few days without breaking the bank.

Your Words: "I wish my apartment was half as nice." "It beats staying at an overpriced, homogenous hotel."

Hotel Belleclaire

250 W 77th Street, Between Broadway & West End Avenue, Manhattan, 212.362.7700, www.hotelbellecairenewyork.com

Hotel Belleclaire was built in 1903 and designed by notable architect E. Roth. The designers of the interior did a fantastic job in maintaining the level of talent that went into building the hotel. Each room is sleek and bright. No tacky paintings on the walls here — the rooms are dominated by one or two colors, and the decoration is minimal but stylish. Most rooms are reasonably large, especially given the price.

The amenities are numerous. Guests can take advantage of a private telephone number, a two-line phone with a dataport and voice mail — advantages you won't find at hotels that charge twice the price. Movies on Demand and cable television are available, as well as Nintendo. Don't get caught obsessing over your favorite video game when you should be outside experiencing the city. 24-hour security is provided, along with an attentive and knowledgeable concierge. The staff is multilingual and helpful. The location is convenient; the hotel is a couple of blocks from the 1/9 subway, which runs along the west side of Manhattan and takes you to Greenwich Village, Tribeca or Midtown in no time flat. Hotel Belleclaire is moderately priced, beautifully decorated and reliable, and a guaranteed positive experience for the adventurous traveler.

Your Words: "Very feng shui! It sure beats the outdated décor at some of the chain hotels." "Great location. I need to be near H & H bagels when I vacation in New York."

Incentra Village House

32 8th Avenue, Between W 12th & Jane Street, Manhattan
212.206.0007

Located on Eighth Avenue in the heart of Greenwich Village and near the subway, Incentra is charming and quiet. These red brick townhouses date back to 1841. Guests are received in the parlor, which features a 1939 Steinway piano (some of the piano bars around town could use that), antique furniture, paintings, and a working fireplace. They then wind their way through narrow halls and stairways to one of 12 suites. Each room is different in size, so ask questions when making reservations, which should be done at least a month in advance. If you prefer a quieter stay, ask for a room in the back. Each room is named for an aspect of the life of Gaylord Hoftiezer, the man who founded the guesthouse. When he passed away, he left the house as a trust. The Washington Room has a loft in addition to a double bed, and is a good choice for a small family. The Garden Room is romantic; it's spacious and of course features a small, well-tended garden with much flora and fauna. Unlike many gay-friendly lodging options in the city, smoking is permitted. Massage is also available, and comes in handy after an arduous day of seeing the sights. For a sense of history and a peaceful vacation, Incentra is a good, gay-friendly lodging choice.

Your Words: "Staying here is a bit of an adventure. The place has a style all its own." "My family takes advantage of the extra space in some of their rooms."

The Inn on 23rd St.

131 W 23rd Street, Between 6th & 7th Avenue, Manhattan
212.463.0330, 877.387.2323

The Inn on 23rd St. truly feels like home away from home, and not in the corny, self-conscious way. Innkeeper Annette Fisherman and her husband sold her Victorian home on Long Island, moved into the city, and furnished the Inn with the eclectic contents of her home. One room is furnished with finds from her old basement: a topographic map hangs on the exposed brick wall, and license plates form the border below the ceiling. The Quilt Room has Mr. Fisherman's grandmother's quilt hanging on the wall, and the Victorian Room contains a romantic canopy bed. Annette oversees the operations daily from the open office in the foyer. She doesn't hide behind a desk, and greets guests with grace and attention.

The rooms are really large by NYC standards, and contain desks, two-line phones with a dataport, and new bathrooms. The library on the second floor and parlor on the first floor are as comfortable as your grandpa's den. Breakfast is served in the morning near the library, and there's an "honor bar" with small liquor bottles. There's also an elevator so you don't have to lug your bags up stairs. If you're visiting, you can't go wrong here. If you're a resident, one look and you'll want to stay here with your main squeeze for the weekend.

Your Words: "I put my family up here when I got married. I think they liked the inn better than the wedding." "The perfect place for business contacts to stay. They're always impressed."

LODGING

Alphabetical Index

INDEX

Neighborhood Index

INDEX